CW01468551

RECIPROCAL TEACHING TECHNIQUES

DR. B. Padma

APH PUBLISHING CORPORATION
4435-36/7, ANSARI ROAD, DARYA GANJ,
NEW DELHI-110 002

Published by

S.B. Nangia
for **APH PUBLISHING CORPORATION**
4435-36/7, Ansari Road,
Darya Ganj,
New Delhi-110 002
Tel.   23274050
        23285807
Fax   91-011-23274050
Email: aphbooks@vsnl.net

2014

© Author

Printed at
Balaji Offset
Navin Shahdara, Delhi-32
Ph.: 22324437

Preface

Reciprocal Teaching is an instructional technique in which students and teacher take turns leading a dialogue about strategies for how to study some material. It is a form of apprenticeship and can be used with various curricula. Reciprocal Teaching parallels the new definition of reading that describes the process as a dynamic interaction between the reader and the text in the reader's attempt to construct meaning from the text. Reciprocal Teaching is a model of constructive learning. The main goal is to promote better Reading comprehension Reciprocal teaching combines different techniques involving the who, what, and where, of learning. Learning groups are formed with a teacher and one or more students. They use a variety of different reading comprehension strategies to study a text passage in different ways. The teacher and students take turns being discussion leaders. The teacher can provide hints, feedback, and comments as needed.

The discovery of Reciprocal Teaching Technique was based on cognitive science research, and its record of validation was *bona fide:* students' reading comprehension improved in every trial and the results remained constant overtime. Among reading experts and practitioners, this technique had been heralded as effective in helping in students improve their reading ability in pre-post trials or research studies. Additionally, Reciprocal Teaching helps novice readers learn and internalize in a short time the strategies excellent readers employ, and they are able to retain the skills and apply them in other content area subjects.

"I realize this technique is for reading books, but I have used something similar to this with my band in reading a new piece of music. It helps the students to predict what a piece by the same composer could be like." *Elizabeth Giger*

"I used reciprocal teaching with my science students also. If we needed to read a passage in the book that might not be too interesting, but they still needed the knowledge. Reciprocal Teaching Technique worked because the students worked in small groups and could concentrate on just a small amount of information, and then they would become the "experts" on what they were to teach their peers." *Sharon Morrisette*

"This is a great way to practice reading strategies in a group."
J. Cappa

"I was not aware of reciprocal teaching until we received professional development on it during my first year of teaching (in 2003). It is now 2006 and I must say that this reading strategy has certainly helped our students. Not only is it useful in the language arts classroom but also in all other subject-areas as well." *Kristy Kleckauskas*

"Reciprocal teaching is the cornerstone of our AP Calculus class. It has been a very positive method in our class."
Brad Frey, Johnsburg High School.

Retrieved from "http://wik.ed.uiuc.edu/index.php/Reciprocal teaching", the above success stories and testimonials impress on us the need to introduce, experiment and apply this innovative teaching technique in Indian Education too. The present study is an earnest effort to experiment and evaluate this Reciprocal Teaching Technique, which has been already popular in developed countries like U.S.A, Canada, U.K., and Spain.

My sincere thanks are to APH Publishing Corporation , New Delhi who have come forward to publish, disseminate and popularise this Innovative Teaching Technique in the form of book, which will contribute to enhancing the Instructional Quality of Indian Education in general and Teacher Education in particular. I am sure, this pioneer contribution will be well-received and widely used by the teachers as well as students.

Dr. B. PADMA

Contents

1
Introduction

"In this era of unprecedented growth in Communication Technology, Economic Change and Social Ferment, there should be such an enormous flow of research in Communication Skills so that the dedicated professionals will keep abreast of latest techniques in this significant field".

International Communication Association, 1999

"A scientist in the West with good Communication Skill earns more than a scientist of more technical knowledge but with less communication skill".

Tickoo, 1998

"Reading proficiency is crucial to success in school and is also essential for economic survival in a technologically oriented world"

Pallncsar & Perry, 1995

"We are men, because we speak. We are cultured, because we read"

Dan Lacy

"Reading maketh a full man"

Francis Bacon

PROLEGOMENON

Reading Education, particularly in early schooling, has been the subject of a host of empirical studies, theoretical accounts and professional recommendations, as well as the topic around which there has been much heated debates. This is partly because of the significance it has assumed in increasingly literacy-dependent curricular programmes (Olson, 1994), and partly because of the economic and cultural importance attributed to literacy by communities and governments (Fuller, Edwards, and Gorman, 1987).

The technologies by which communication skills in general and reading skills in particular are taught and evaluated have proved a fascinating puzzle to Language Teachers, Administrators and Research Scholars. It has absorbed the scientific lifetime of technologists and linguists and has been accorded more than passing interest by evaluation specialists and psycholinguists. But unfortunately there is very little volume of research and publications in this vital area.

Interest in communication skills has increased dramatically since social scientists first turned their attention to life skills in the mid-1960s. But "overall understanding of communication skills has not reached a level where prescriptive generalizations are warranted". (The International Encyclopaedia of Education, 1988). Communication skills, a subset of general social skills, are concerned with the manipulation of symbols for the accomplishment of some purpose. "The concept underlying both teaching and research in this area is that pupils vary in their ability to communicate with others, and that by improving their skills, they will have more effective and satisfying communication experiences." (The International Encyclopaedia of Linguistics, 1992). The term 'Communicative Competence' was coined by Delltynes in 1966, in a proposal to broaden the scope of knowledge and skills embodied in Noam Chomsky's definition of 'Linguistic Competence' in 1965. Attempts to reach agreement on the scope of 'Communicative Competence' have not been successful although the use of the term has become widespread across disciplines. The assessment of communication skills is approached from three points of view:

1.   First, the several abilities that constitute communication skills are examined.

2.   Then, the different tasks that may be defined as communication tests are considered.

3.   Finally, populations to be tested are taken into account.

Man, as social being, lives in a society, conveying his thoughts and ideas to one another. Language is the instrument through which ideas are transmitted from one mind to another. Language is a system of communication and as such it is essential for human society and every society has its own language.

All living creatures have some means of conveying information to their own group; communication is ultimately essential for their survival. In this regard, some use vocal voices, others physical movements and others facial expressions. Man is unique in the sense that he was created in a very complex way. A comprehensive system of communication, therefore, unlike the sign and symbols, which are the modes of learning of the birds and animals, needs a language.

Language primarily means speech. The word 'language' comes from the Latin word 'lingua' which means 'tongue' and its original meaning is that 'which is produced with tongue'. Language is not only speech but also writing, pictures, symbols that catch the eye, like green traffic lights, etc. Language is a structural system of arbitrary sounds and sound sequences, which is used in communication and which is fairly a complete catalogue of the things, events and process in a given environment. Language is a means through which interaction between human beings takes place and without language there could be no culture. Language is like a diamond that reveals the light in even, varying gleams from its numerous facets.

COMMUNICATION SKILL - A THEORETICAL FRAMEWORK

Communication, the exchange of meanings between individuals through a common system of symbols, has been of concern to countless scholars since the time of ancient Greece. Until recently, however, the topic was usually subsumed under other disciplines and taken for granted as a natural process inherent to each human being. In 1928, the English literary critic and author I.A.Richards offered one of the first and in some ways still the best definitions of communication as "a discrete aspect of human enterprise".

Communication takes place when one mind so acts upon its environment that another mind is influenced, and in that other mind an experience occurs which is like the experience in the first mind, and is caused in part by that experience.

The early meaning of communication derived from the Latin word, 'communicare' which means 'to make common' has undergone many changes. These changes have made its meaning broader and complicated as well.

For example, the early Bullet Theory (Schramm, 1971) conceived communication as a process of transferring feelings, motivations, ideas and knowledge from one mind to another, in a way in which the receiver was seen as a passive agent. This was the situation assumed in the post-World War I propaganda and the Nazi propaganda in Germany. In his view, "Communication is the sharing of an orientation toward a set of informational signs". Information refers to not only facts/news or whatever is taught as the "silent language'. This communication is based on machines-that are 'in-tune' with each other. This relationship may not be face-to-face, for example in case of mass media.

But the quality of communication in direct contact differs from that of indirect or mediated contact. Communication is an activity, which is not limited to any static condition. One 'learns' how to communicate, and for this learning, one uses communication itself. This is the process that goes on in the schools and colleges of today.

EDUCATIONAL POLICY AND LANGUAGE INSTRUCTION

Educational policy is deeply influenced by language attitudes, for language is a central mediating factor in education (Kelly, 1969). Schools, universities and institutions of further education are thus determined by language(s) and attitudes towards language. This occurs in several ways:

❖ through the language(s) of instruction chosen or prescribed

❖ through contact with other languages in use within the broader environment of a given educational institution (e.g., the mother tongue of pupils and students where these differ from the local language)

India is a vast country consisting of various languages. There are eighteen national languages recognized by the Indian constitution as given below:

1.	Assamese	7.	Konkani	13.	Punjabi
2.	Bengali	8.	Malayalam	14.	Sanskrit
3.	Gujarathi	9.	Manipuri	15.	Sindhi
4.	Hindi	10.	Marathi	16.	Tamil
5.	Kannada	11.	Nepali	17.	Telugu
6.	Kashmiri	12.	Oriaya	18.	Urdu

FOUR FOLD ANALYSIS OF THE LANGUAGE SKILLS

The communicative approach to language teaching aims at learner-centered materials for the development of four major skills, viz., Listening, Speaking, Reading and Writing. Harris (1974), an outstanding expert in the testing of languages has observed, "Language exists in two forms, the spoken and the written. Two linguistic activities are associated with both speech and writing - an encoding and a decoding process. Speaking and writing themselves are the encoding processes whereby we communicate our ideas, thoughts, or feelings through one or the other form of language;

and listening and reading are the parallel decoding processes by which we comprehend either a spoken or a written message. Thus, language includes four skills or complexes of skills - listening, speaking, reading and writing. It is perhaps in this order that we originally learnt our native language, and it is in that order that foreign languages are now very frequently taught and tested."

A four-fold analysis of language skills is given in Figure 1.

		ASPECT	
		1. Skills of Comprehension	2. Skills of Expression
		Receptive/Passive	Productive/Active
(a)	Spoken Medium	Listening	Speaking
(b)	Written Medium	Reading	Writing

Fig 1.1 Four fold analysis of the language skills

SPECIAL PLACE OF READING IN THE COMPLEXITY OF LANGUAGE SKILLS

Reading occupies a special place in the complexity of language skills, which are listening, speaking, writing and spelling. Reading is the process of using one's eyes and mind to understand the literal as well as the hidden meaning of what the writer was attempting to convey. Reading is the process of coming in to contact with the minds of millions of wise men and women, dead or alive, who have recorded their experiences for the readers' benefit. As a means of communication reading is more versatile than wireless and television, not to mention the telegraph, the telephone, and the teletype. It is many things to many people. It is a telescope, because through it we can look at the distant stars and speculate about the life upon them. It is a microscope because through it we can not only examine the chromosomes and the atoms, but also infer these minute particles, which even the finest lenses cannot reveal. It is a never- ending wide screen film on which the human past passes in review. It is the only known time machine that can recreate the events of the past and open up the vistas of the future.

Stevenson (1997) states that, "Reading takes us out of our country and ourselves. Reading is a process, which helps one to understand the world".

According to Francis Keppel (1994), "Every examination of the problems of our schools, of poverty; every question raised by troubled parents about our schools, every learning disorder seems to show some association with reading difficulty."

IMPORTANCE OF READING

In the fast changing world today, educational institutions are confronted with the demand that they prepare the students directly for living. They must be helped to develop the intellectual and emotional capacities for a happy and socially, useful life. They must be given the knowledge, the skills, and the flexibility, which will enable them to meet unprecedented and unpredictable problems. They need to understand themselves; they need to work out relationships with other people. Above all, they must achieve some philosophy, some inner center from which to view in perspective the shuffling society and its future development. To have pragmatic value, any knowledge about man and society that the schools can give them must make them fit for a decent society, and must be assimilated into the stream of their actual life.

In olden days, knowledge was passed on from father to son and the Gurukula method of teaching was followed. But they are not applicable or suitable to the modern world and situation today. Books are the most valuable treasure houses of knowledge. The men of past, since the dawn of civilization, had left the footprints of all the varied experiences they had. The men of today can acquire them all by reading these books. Those literatures of the past not only guide them but also warn them of their forthcoming dangers.

It is a fact that there are many problems worrying the world of today. The printed materials not only bring us news of the problems of today but they also recount the problems of the ages and the ideas, which have been offered as solutions to those problems. At least a partial solution to these problems may be obtained from gleaming clues from history, from the way similar problems have been handled in other times.

"Reading is to the mind what exercise is to the body," says Richard Steel, a 17th century writer. The efficiency and ability to read play an important role in the life of a student. So considerable amount of time of the students can be utilized to cultivate in them the habit of reading, which will enable them to personal and social adjustments.

READING - A CONCEPTUAL DEFINITION

Reading is not merely recognizing the printed symbols and

pronouncing the words correctly. It is not merely, being able to reproduce verbatim or in summarized form what the author has stated. Reading is more than seeing words clearly, more than pronouncing printed words correctly, more than recognizing the meaning of individual words. Reading requires one to think, feel and use one's imagination. Effective reading is purposeful. The use one makes of one's reading largely determines what one reads, why one reads and how one reads.

OBJECTIVES OF READING
The objectives of reading are:

1. To increase vocabulary and word perception skills.
2. To improve word study skills.
3. To critically evaluate what is read.
4. To improve basic comprehension skills.
5. To develop more natural reading interests and tastes.

Even though high school students may have been exposed to an excellent reading program in the elementary grades, it is presumptuous to assume that all previously taught skills have been mastered - even by the average or bright students. Excellent instruction would be expected to increase the range of performance among the students, poor instruction to reduce not only the range of individual differences but also the level of performance.

SPEED AND COMPREHENSION IN READING
Reading performance is usually assessed in terms of two aspects - speed and comprehension. Teachers at all educational levels, elementary school through college are under pressure to improve their students reading speed and comprehension.

The only justifiable or valid definition of 'Speed of Reading' is 'Speed of Comprehension'. Reading without comprehension is not reading. Every teacher should keep in mind that rapid reading in itself is not a cause of better understanding. A fast rate of comprehension becomes possible only because the pupil possesses the ability necessary for clear and rapid understanding.

Venkata Iyer (1986) evolved the following formula to arrive at the speed-reading coefficient of the subjects:

$$\text{Speed in words per minute} = \frac{\text{No. of words in the passage} \times 60}{\text{Time taken in second}}$$

Comprehension scores are arrived at by many researchers in reading by giving one score for each correct answer to the objective type of test items given with the passage.

Unfortunately, the exact relationships between speed of reading and comprehension are not firmly established. This condition is due to poorly designed experimentations.

TYPES OF READING

The traditional and popular classifications of reading are Oral Reading and Silent Reading. There are also some special types of reading which have gained much prominence today and they are known as Skimming, Cursory Reading, Study Reading and Critical Reading.

(a) Oral Reading

Even though the major emphasis in reading today, is on silent reading, children need to become good oral readers. Pupils benefit by reading aloud prose, poetry or drama. Oral Reading leads to better appreciation of literature, improvement in pronunciation, phrasing, rhythm and flexibility.

Oral reading also has social values. It provides enjoyment in social group, helps and lets one share content to which all do not have access and is useful in making reports and announcements, and presenting other information to a group.

Oral reading requires all the sensory and perceptual skills required in silent reading such as visual discrimination, rhythmic progression along a line of print and the ability to take to the word those experiences that the writer, by his/her peculiar choice and arrangement of words, hoped to call to the readers' attention. Oral reading also requires skills beyond those needed in silent reading.

(b) Silent Reading

Habits of oral reading usually are quite different from those in silent reading. The child who exercises great care in oral reading may pass over the difficult words in silent reading. In oral reading, there are generally more fixations, more regressions and longer pauses. Oral reading is generally slower than silent reading. In oral reading, the rate of speed is limited by pronunciation. In silent reading, it is limited only by the ability to grasp meaning. Oral reading calls for interpreting to others, silent reading only to oneself. Oral reading demands skills in voice, tone and pause and in sensing the mood and feelings intended by the author.

(c) Skimming

The most rapid kind of reading consists of merely looking for key words. The purpose of skimming is to locate the exact place where information may be found, to obtain a general survey or birds-eye view of a longer section before settling down to read it carefully, or to determine whether the section is relevant to the problem under consideration. Skimming is often helpful in getting them to skip around in the print. Skimming contributes to good study habits, for it saves time and energy and facilitates the location of pertinent information.

(d) Cursory Reading

Cursory reading also is used at all grade levels. In this type of reading, pupils read through once as rapidly as they can to make selection. Skipping over unknown words is done to obtain a general over view or the main idea. This is similar to skimming but it requires the reading of main units in more details than skimming does. Cursory reading is also useful as a review of previously read material in order to make a summary.

(e) Study Reading

Study reading is another type of reading to which the rate of speed must be adjusted according to the grade level of the students. This type of reading is done to obtain the greatest possible understanding such as reading to visualize a scene, to comprehend directions, to follow arguments, to make an outline, to prepare a play, to get information or to take an open book examination.

(f) Critical Reading

Critical reading begins in the primary grades when children are given a chance to relate what they have read to their own experiences. Secondary school students delve into the whole realm of adult writing. They are faced with even more complex patterns of style.

In each of the types of reading discussed above, teachers should encourage students to read at their optimum rate without comprehension loss while the improvement of rate of reading is not the crucial skill in the elementary school. But increased speed in reading becomes important in secondary schools and colleges. Nevertheless, attention to the above types of reading and to the purpose of each should enable a student in adjusting the rate of speed for each purpose, which in turn will improve his/her study habits.

IMPORTANCE OF READING IN THE MODERN WORLD

It is normal that every teacher and the parent expect their children to be a good reader. Because reading is considered as one of the most important abilities in the educational development today, mastery of reading is unavoidable in learning all the school subjects. But adequate attention is not given to this aspect today. According to Witty Paul (1986), "An ordinary reader reads at 150 to 180 words per minute and understand 50 to 60% of the ideas presented".

How fast a person can read depends on the individual. A good reader may be able to read a thousand words per minute, but he won't use the speed on every thing he reads. A good reader reads his/her social science text at rates between 400 and 500 words per minute. But it may take him/her 150 words per minute to read his/her science or mathematics text. A good reader may read newspaper and magazine articles at 600 words per minute, but a poem may even need to be read aloud and faster.

DIFFERENT PERCEPTIONS OF READING

Reading has been viewed from different points of view and each of these views deals with different dimensions and different characteristics of reading.

(a) Reading as a Sensory Process

Reading requires the use of the senses, especially vision. The reader must react visually to the graphic symbols. They symbols themselves must be legible. The eyes must see clearly and the light must be adequate.

(b) Reading as a Perceptual Process

Reading occurs when meaning is brought to graphic stimuli. It is progressive acquisition of the meaning and ideas represented by a sequence of words. It includes seeing the word, recognition of the word, awareness of the word's meaning and reflecting the word to its context. This is perception in its fullest sense.

(c) Reading as a Response

Reading is a system of responses made to some graphic stimuli. These include the vocal and or sub-vocal muscular responses made at sight of the word.

The eye movements during reading involves physical adaptations to the reading act such as postural changes, the critical and evaluative responses to what is being read, the emotional involvement of the reader and meaningful reactions to the word.

(d) Reading as a Learned Process

Reading is a response that must be learned by the child and it is under the control of the mechanism of motivation and reinforcement.

(e) Reading as a Development Task

Any development task has one basic characteristic - the child's readiness which, depends on the child's general development. Reading is a difficult task and there is a most teachable moment for beginning reading and for each of the specific skills in reading. The child's level of achievement in reading depends on his over all growth and development.

(f) Reading as a Joyous Activity

Reading may become an interesting activity or a goal in its right. It then may motivate other activities too. Reading is a favourite pastime in many cultures and for people of all ages. Reading can transform one's outlook on life and give a whole wonderful view on living. Reading is a door to a world of wonder.

(g) Reading as a Learning Process

Reading may become one of the chief media for learning. The child can use reading to acquire knowledge and to change his own attitudes ideas and aspirations. Genuine reading involves integration and promotes the development of the reader. It opens up to him a world of ideas, takes him to distant lands and lets him walk side by side with the great sages of time.

(h) Reading as Communication

Reading is an active process. Communication from writer to reader occurs only if the reader can take meaning to the printed page. The reader interprets what he read in the light of his background, associates it with past experience and projects beyond it in terms of ideas, judgements, applications and conclusions.

IMPROVING READING SPEED

One reads not only with the eyes but with the brain too. Fast reading is only possible when one is already familiar with the language and its content. The rules and grammatical sequences of languages enable one to anticipate what is coming, next in the text.

There are two main sorts of difficulties in reading.

1. Slow movement of eyes
2. Difficulties in understanding arising from a poor vocabulary or lack of familiarity with the material.

The specific defects found in the younger readers include excessive word analysis and word by word reading, lip movement and sub-vocal movements, difficulties with the return sweep, regression back along the line and slowness in word recognition. These defects are not very common or severe in older students.

FACTORS AFFECTING READING

It has been established well that there are several factors, which have direct or indirect influence on the speed of reading. The following are some of them.

(a) Adequate Experiential Background

Experience is the basis for all the educational development. The symbols on the page are empty unless the reader endows them with meaning. For this, the pupil needs the appropriate experience.

(b) Adequate Language Background

Reading is a language experience and progress in reading occurs most readily when it is taught as one phase of the total communication process. So a common cause for poor reading is poor language ability.

(c) Listening Ability

The ability to listen is an important effect on the development of competency in reading. Listening provides the vocabulary and the sentence structure. Ability to listen is a good indicator of potential progress in reading.

(d) Maturation

The pupils' achievements depend as much as maturation as on experience. Maturation is an unfolding or 'ripening' of potentials that an individual possesses by virtue of his being a member of a given species or more specifically by virtue of his biological inheritance from a particular heritage.

(e) Intellectual Development

Success in reading is built upon certain intellectual skills. The pupils must perceive likeness and difference, must be able to recognize word form and must possess certain thinking skills. They must have developed an appropriate memory and attention span. Besides these, there are other factors like mental age, motivation, instructional procedure, etc., which influence reading.

There are other factors related to the mechanics of reading, which affect the reading efficiency of individuals. They are vocalization, sub-vocalization, supports, head movements, word-by-word reading and regression. Bayley (1957), Guy L. Bond and Miles. A.Tinker (1957),

Norman Lewis (1980), Manya and Eric DeLeeuw (1983), Venkata Iyer (1986), G.C.Ahuja and Pramila Ahuja (1987), Pramila Ahuja and G.C.Ahuja (1991) have made detailed studies of the factors and enlisted these factors into certain categories on the basis of the nature of impediment involved.

READING RESEARCH

The history of education has witnessed ceaseless efforts to bring about a lasting relationship between the human child and the printed language. This explains why much of reading research has been carried out at elementary level students.

Reading research during the past twenty years has been characterized by simultaneous efforts at many fronts. These new areas in reading research imply a shift from its earlier focuses. Contemporary reading research is now concerned with

(a) The role of cognitive processes in reading

(b) The nature of reading comprehension and

(c) The models of reading and component skills of the reading process (Veena Sabharwal, 1992)

Many research studies have been conducted to evolve a reading development strategy or set of strategies that would raise the reading levels of students. One such research was carried out in 1987 by Anne Marie Palinscar, from Michigan State University and Anne Brown, from the University of Illinois and the outcome was the discovery of Reciprocal Teaching. The application of Reciprocal Teaching strategy was experimented on urban students in Highland Park, Michigan, and the success of the above experiment was reported by UNESCO-International Bureau of Education in 2001 in its *"Innodata Monographs - 8"*

RECIPROCAL TEACHING - HISTORICAL BACKGROUND

The discovery of Reciprocal Teaching was based on cognitive science research, and its record of validation was bonafide; student-reading comprehension improved in every trial and the results remained constant over time. Among reading experts and practitioners, the technique had been heralded as effective in helping students improve their reading ability in pre-post trials or research studies (Pearson & Doyle 1987; Pressley, Snyder & Cariglia-Bull, 1987). Additionally, Bruer (1993) reported that Reciprocal Teaching helps novice readers learn and internalize in a short time the strategies excellent readers employ, and they are able to retain the skills and apply them in other content area subjects. That the technique was short in duration, twenty days, was also part of its appeal.

Origins of Reciprocal Teaching

Bruer (1993) traces the cognitive science research related to Reciprocal Teaching and tells the story of its evolution as a comprehension-fostering strategy. According to Bruer, Anne-Marrie Palinscar, co-creator of Reciprocal Teaching reviewed Meichenbaum's (1985) self-verbalization techniques, which had demonstrated success with impulsive children, to determine whether they could be useful in regulating children's cognitive processing, particularly those that impact and result in reading competence. Meichenbaum suggested that Palinscar strengthen self-verbalization by incorporating ideas on research on meta-cognition and referred her to Ann Brown, an expert on meta-cognition.

RECIPROCAL TEACHING - A CONCEPTUAL FRAMEWORK

'Reciprocal Teaching' is an instructional procedure designed to enhance reading comprehension in young (elementary and middle school) students. It is characterized by

- ❖ Dialogue between students and teacher, each taking a turn in the role of a dialogue leader.
- ❖ 'Reciprocal': Interactions where one person acts in response to the other.
- ❖ Structured dialogue using four strategies / steps viz., Predicting, Summarizing, Questioning and Clarifying.

According to Palincsar (1986) " Reciprocal teaching refers to an instructional activity that takes place in the form of a dialogue between teachers and students regarding segments of text. The dialogue is structured by the use of four strategies: predicting, summarizing, question generating and clarifying. The teacher and students take turns assuming the role of teacher in leading this dialogue. The purpose of reciprocal teaching is to facilitate a group effort between teacher and students as well as among students in the task of bringing meaning to the text."

Reciprocal Teaching is characterized as a dialogue, taking place between the teacher and students (or student leader and members of the group) that results in students learning how to construct meaning when they are placed in must-read situations (tests or assignments). The approach derives from the theory that reading for meaning and retention — what is referred to as study reading-requires effort, a full repertoire of comprehension strategies (namely, summarizing, generating questions, clarifying and predicting), and the flexibility to use these strategies, as the situation requires. Each of the strategies helps students to construct meaning from text and monitor their reading to ensure that they in fact understand what they read. These strategies inform them when they have wandered off, missed the point, are confused, cannot predict what is coming up, or are not following the gist of that to be learned (Bruer, 1993)

Reciprocal Teaching thus parallels the new definition of reading that describes the process as a dynamic interaction between the reader and the text in the reader's attempt to construct meaning from the text. Using prior experience as a channel, readers learn new information, main ideas, make connections, and generally make sense from the text as intended by the author. Readers construct meaning by relying on prior experience to parallel, contract or affirm what the author suggests. All excellent readers do this construction. Otherwise, the content would be meaningless alphabetic squiggles on the page. Without meaning construction, learning does not take place. Reciprocal Teaching is a model of constructivist learning.

STRATEGIES OF RECIPROCAL TEACHING

Each of the four strategies of Reciprocal Teaching helps students construct meaning from text and monitor their reading to ensure that they in fact understand what they read.

Predicting requires the readers to hypothesize about what the author might discuss next in the text. This is an opportunity for the students to link the new knowledge they will encounter in the text with the knowledge they already process. It also enables the students to understand the structure of the text. Additionally, with predicting, an opportunity has been created for the readers to link the new knowledge they were encountered in the text to the knowledge they already possess. It also facilitates the use of text structure as students learn that headings, sub-headings and questions in the text are useful means of anticipating what might occur next. To predict, the reader must read with anticipation and expectancy, watching for text clues indicating where the author is going next. The inability to predict may also be an indicator that comprehension is inadequate.

Summarizing provides the students with opportunity to identify, paraphrase and integrate important information in the text. It requires the reader to recall and state that gist he/she has constructed. Therefore, a reader who can summarize has activated background knowledge to integrate information appearing in the text, allocated attention to the main points, and evaluated the gist for consistency. The inability of the reader to summarize text indicates that comprehension is incomplete.

Questioning helps the students identify the kind of information significant enough to form the basis for a question. It is also a form of self-test. Generating questions about text, likewise, depends on the gist and the function needed for summarizing, but with one additional demand: that the reader monitors the gist to pick out the important points. To generate questions, the reader is required to re-process the information read into question format. The inability to formulate appropriate questions about text is another indicator that comprehension has not occurred.

Clarifying enables the students to identify the difficulties in comprehending the text and the reasons for the same. They also conclude whether to reread a segment of the text, or to go ahead or to ask for help. When a reader clarifies the point, he/she must allocate attention to the difficult points and engage in critical evaluation of the gist. In short, clarifying directs the reader to look for parts of the passage that are confusing and unclear. The reader must ask the question: 'Is there anything in this segment that I don't understand?' If there are unclear segments which block understanding, the reader is signaled to re-read, read ahead or ask for help.

Although Palinscar and Brown's original study involved seventh grade. English speakers who were recognized as having poor comprehension skills, the reciprocal teaching protocol is applicable wherever readers are vulnerable to comprehension failure. Reciprocal teaching is introduced as a strategy to improve student comprehension of the text while involving them in a verbal exchange of ideas. Students "reciprocate" their skills, experiences, and understanding as they follow the model.

The process begins with the instructor modeling the steps of Reciprocal Teaching. The instructor reads the title and subtitle of the text segment and raises questions as to what might be covered in the text. Then the passage is read and the points are summed up at every point of transition. Next the instructor asks the students a question to which the students respond orally. The students ask a question of the instructor about the text for the purpose of clarification. The process is repeated by the instructor until students are familiar with the sequence of activities and the skills involved. A student then performs the modeling role in either a large group or in small groups or pairs with the instructor acting as "coach," ultimately withdrawing from the process.

RESEARCH IN RECIPROCAL TEACHING
Palincsar and Brown (1985) conducted a series of studies to determine the effectiveness of reciprocal teaching. The initial studies were

conducted by adult tutors working with middle school students in pairs and teachers working with their small reading groups averaging five in number. The students were identified to be fairly adequate decoders but very poor comprehenders, typically performing at least two years below grade level on standardized measures of comprehension. Instruction took place over a period of 20 consecutive school days. The effectiveness was evaluated by having the students read passages about 450 to 500 words in length and answer 10 comprehension questions from recall. The students completed five of these passages before reciprocal teaching instruction began and one during each day of instruction. Performance on these assessment passages indicated that all but one of the experimental students achieved criterion performance, which was identified as 70 percent accuracy for four out of five consecutive days.

These results were in contrast to the group of control students, none of whom achieved criterion performance. In addition, qualitative changes were observed in the dialogue that occurred daily. For example, the experimental students functioned more independently of the teachers and improved the quality of their summaries over time. In addition, students' ability to write summaries, predict the kinds of question teachers and tests ask, and detect incongruities in text improved. Finally, these improvements were reflected in the regular classroom as the experimental students' percentile rankings went from 20 to 50 and above on texts administered in social studies and science classes.

When the same instructional procedure was implemented in larger classes with groups ranging in size from 8 to 18, 71 percent of the students achieved criterion performance as opposed to 19 percent of the control students who were involved in individualized skill instruction. Furthermore, teachers observed fewer behavioural problems in their reciprocal teaching groups than in their control groups."

REFLECTIONS ON THE RECIPROCAL TEACHING MODEL

The primary benefit of this reading strategy is that comprehension is likely to increase (Palinscar and Brown 1984, 1987, Gilory and Moore 1986), but there are a number of other advantages.

  ◈   Initially, while the instructor is responsible for predicting, summarizing, questioning and clarifying and students are able to observe and question the skills performed by an "expert". This allows the instructor to explain how the skills originate in the reading experience. In this way, both cognitive and meta-cognitive awareness of reading comprehension is attended to.

Through Reciprocal Teaching, learners become aware of their "cognitive resources" and their "self regulatory mechanism" which they use in their efforts to understand what they read. "What a reader knows about the task of reading will influence how he/she sets about controlling reading activities." (Brown, 1982)

◈ Students practise four basic reading skills and test their ideas against those of their peers. At the same time, they are listening and speaking in an authentic academic setting. They employ interactive techniques that are linguistically appropriate (interrupting gambits, question formation, opinion statements, agreement/disagreement phrases) and socially appropriate (taking turns, interpreting body language, and sharing responsibility).

◈ Students' vocabulary needs are contextualized and clarified, and opportunities exist for using relevant vocabulary during discussion of the text.

◈ The students' independence from the classroom teacher encourages autonomy in the reading process.

◈ A video of students engaged in Reciprocal Teaching provides data for the analysis of reading skills and group dynamics.

◈ Skills are transferable to the reading of texts across the disciplines.

◈ The Reciprocal Teaching reading group forms a natural study group.

Reciprocal Teaching is easy to follow, reinforces skills that are basic to reading successfully and provides a forum for the integration of communicative activities. Its potential for multilevel and cross-discipline application makes this model a valuable teaching tool in the language classroom.

NEED FOR THE PRESENT STUDY

Though teachers and educationists are quite aware of the importance of reading, yet very little has been done to develop the skill in reading to the desired level. In western countries, teachers, educationists and parents can assess and evaluate the progress of their wards at every step with the help of standardized test on reading to suit different grades and age levels and adopt suitable remedial measures. But in India, such steps are very few in number and often quite unsuitable to Indian needs, as India is a vast and growing country differing in every respect from one part to another, in language, culture and so on. Especially no such remedial measures and reading improvement strategies are available in India, In the rapidly changing political, economic and social life of India, there is a renewed emphasis on and search for, cultural identity. An important factor in all this is language which is a veritable vehicle for culture and tradition. Since mother tongue education constitutes a "renewal of connection" with a people's language and cultural heritage, it is to be expected that its importance in educational planning and policy will continue to increase. A continuing study of the practices, techniques, new developments and experiments in mother tongue education will therefore continue to be a worthwhile investment. Studies abstracted in the Six surveys of Research in Education (1974, 1979, 1986, 1991, 1996 and 2000) reveal that no research was undertaken with a focus on reciprocal teaching in terms of the students' communicative competence. While the studies of Devanathan (1988) and Selvaraj Gnanaguru (1994) are related to Reading skills in Tamil at elementary and high school level, the present study is unique and different from them as it attempts to study the effect of Reciprocal Teaching, as a reading improvement techniques. Reciprocal Teaching has aroused international interest. The North Central Regional Educational Laboratory, an educational resource laboratory, has a web site that explains Reciprocal Teaching and summarizes the research from which it comes. The University of Washington posts a Reciprocal Teaching Home Page that reviews the research and concluded that the technique is effective. In fact, an Internet search to locate Reciprocal Teaching resources received 122,000 sites on date. Another example includes the European Union: Challenges to integrate, which integrates both higher-order thinking skills and Reciprocal Teaching. In Canada, Hewitt (1995) published a review of Reciprocal Teaching that concludes that the technique is attractive for its simplicity of form and success in realizing its goals. A review of related literature and research studies conducted in India reveals a research gap that no study has been conducted to test the effectiveness of Reciprocal Teaching in the Indian context with a focus of improving reading in Tamil at the elementary level. Hence, the present investigation has been undertaken to apply Reciprocal Teaching as a reading improvement technique and to find out its effectiveness in raising the reading comprehension of the elementary level students.

SCOPE OF THE STUDY

The present experiment on Reciprocal Teaching was begun with the following scope in mind: to ensure that students poor in reading skill received instruction in monitoring and regulating their reading comprehension; to help teachers realize first- hand the benefit of small-group dialogues as vehicles of comprehension because these matched the new definition of reading exactly; and to encourage a new basic requirement among teachers -proficiency in using Reciprocal Teaching Technique. A system was developed by the investigator for introducing Reciprocal Teaching. The procedure arrived at in the study for educating the effectiveness of Reciprocal Teaching is worthy of mention in the Indian context. Research studies conducted abroad suggest that Reciprocal Teaching is effective in helping students improve their reading ability in pre-post trials or research studies. However, there have been no conclusive evidences that the Reciprocal Teaching is an effective intervention in the Indian context. The present study which establishes the effectiveness of Reciprocal Teaching as a reading improvement strategy could help decision makers to apply this strategy on Indian students who are poor in reading at a wider level. The Reciprocal Teaching Technique would provide with a model, which could be used to teach teachers and parents on how to promote reading comprehension among the students. Teachers, parents and administrators capitalize on this strategy on a variety of fronts: as a mechanism to develop staff for the use of Reciprocal Teaching methods: as a technique through which the parents and students could be taught alike and as a technique that the Government and Management schools could teach to classroom teachers to ensure the likelihood of more widespread application.

STATEMENT OF THE PROBLEM

In a multilingual country like India, the role of the first language in the educational scenario has been subjected to long ranging hot discussions at various levels. In this connection, the clear and emphatic opinions of Gandhiji are still relevant: "*I must not be understood to decry English or its noble literature. The columns of the HARIJAN are sufficient evidence of my love of English. However virile the English language may be, it can never become the language of the masses of India. The foreign medium has caused brain fag, put an undue strain upon the nerves of our children, made them crammers and imitators, unfitted them for original work and thought and disabled them for filtrating their learning to the family or the masses. The foreign medium has prevented the growth of our vernaculars. If I had the powers of a despot, I would today stop the tuition of boys and girls through a foreign medium, and require all the teachers and professors on pain or dismissal to introduce the change forthwith. It is an evil that needs a summary remedy. I must cling to my mother tongue as to my mother's breast, in spite of its shortcomings. It alone can give me the life-giving milk". (Young India-1-10-1928).*

At present in the Indian sub continent, where 840 million people use over 1650 languages and dialects including more than 200 classified languages and 18 constitutionally recognized languages of national importance, the role of mother tongue should be appreciated properly. In India, the Central Institute of English and Foreign Languages (CIEFL), the National Council of Educational Research and Training (NCERT) and the Regional Institute of English (RIE) are working towards improving the standard of English. But there are no such agencies for mother tongue in the State of Tamil Nadu. The teachers of mother tongue are in a sort of isolation, in the total absence of any professional support from the agencies of education, which gives a closed professional atmosphere and makes it a static system. It is unfortunate that there is no empirical evidence to ascertain the effectiveness of Reciprocal Teaching in the Indian cultural context at elementary level in line with the above issues and concerns, the present study entitled "Reciprocal Teaching as a Technique of Improving Reading at the Elementary Level" has been undertaken.

OPERATIONAL DEFINITION OF TERMS

By the term "Reciprocal Teaching", the investigator means an instructional technique designed to enhance reading comprehension among elementary school students during which four comprehension strategies are actively employed namely prediction, questioning, summarizing and clarifying. These four strategies are directly presented, explained and modeled by the teacher. Once students are comfortable with the strategies, they are invited to become "the teacher" and conduct Reciprocal Teaching dialogues with new text material. At this point the teacher's role shifts from providing direct instruction to monitoring progress and providing feedback. With increasing competence, students are given greater independence from the teacher to work in pairs to coach one another, predict, summarize, ask questions, clarify and think aloud about what they are reading

By the term "Reading", the investigator means a very complex process in which the recognition and comprehension of written symbols are influenced by the perceptual skills, the word analysis skill, the experience, the language background, the mind set and the reading ability of the reader, as he anticipates meaning on the basis of what he has just read. The total process is a Gestalt or a whole in which a serious flaw in any major function or part may prevent adequate information. Reading Comprehension is an umbrella term under which a number of basic abilities are often presented, For the purpose of the present study, an attempt has been made to improve the Reading Speed, Reading Comprehension and Vocabulary acquisition of the elementary school students.

By the term "Elementary Level", the investigator means the significant stage of Tamil Nadu School Education system consisting of standards VI, VII and VIII in which pre adolescent pupils of the age group between 11 to 13 study.

OBJECTIVES OF THE STUDY

The main objective of the present experimental study was to find out the effectiveness of Reciprocal Teaching of reading over the conventional method of teaching and reading to the students of 8th Standard. The experiment was designed and carried out to find out answers to the following questions:

1.   Is there any advantage in favour of the experimental or control group with regard to the comparison of reading improvement at the elementary level?

2.   Is there any significant difference in the reading comprehension level as a result of Reciprocal Teaching, of the sub-samples based on Sex, Locality, Type of Management, Socio-Economic Status, Exposure to Newspapers and Magazines and Language Interest?

Finding answers to the above questions required the formulation of specific objectives for the experiment in a more precise, research-oriented style as given below:

1.   To compare the mean Reading Comprehension scores of Experimental Group and Control Group.

2.   To compare the mean gain scores of Experimental Group and Control Group for the total sample and sub samples.

3.   To qualitatively analyses the effect of Reciprocal Teaching Technique on teachers and students.

4.   To offer suggestions and recommendations on the basis of the findings of the experiment.

HYPOTHESES

The specific hypotheses formulated on the basis of the insights gained from the review of related literature and tested by the experiment are given below:

1. There will be significant difference between the mean achievement scores of the Experimental and Control Group students in the sub tests on Reading Comprehension, Reading Speed and Vocabulary.

2. Pupils taught through Reciprocal teaching Technique will have high mean achievement than that of pupils taught through Conventional Methods of Teaching.

VARIABLES TAKEN FOR THE STUDY

In the words of Garret, 1971, "The term Variables' refers to attributes or qualities which exhibit differences in magnitude and which vary along some dimensions". The students' improvement of the Reading Skills is caused, promoted and affected by various variables, like variables arising out of the person, variables arising out of the home, variables arising out of their parents, etc.

(a) Independent Variables

Reciprocal Teaching Technique and Conventional Method of Teaching were the independent variables.

(b) Dependent Variables

Reading Comprehension Score, Reading Speed Score and Vocabulary Test Score were considered as the dependent variables.

(c) Basal Variables

Sex of the Sample, Type of Management, Locality, Socio-Economic Status, Exposure to Newspaper and Magazines and Language Interest were the basal variables for the study.

(d) Control of Intervening and Extraneous Variables

Randomization, Matching the two groups and Statistical balancing were the procedures adopted for controlling the confounding variables.

METHODOLOGY OF THE STUDY

Two groups of Std. VIII pupils were equated on the basis of pre-test score to form the experimental and control groups. One group was treated as Reciprocal Teaching Group (RTG), which was taught through reciprocal teaching technique. The other group was treated as Conventional Method Group (CMC), which was taught through conventional method of teaching.

SAMPLE FOR THE STUDY

Pre-test Post-test Equivalent-Groups Design was adopted for the study in which, the participants were randomly assigned either the experimental group or the control group.

Two intact groups of Std. VIII pupils from two section each in Ten elementary schools were taken as experimental group and control group. Due representation was given to rural-urban locality of the schools, type of management and sex of the students. The experiment was conducted on a sample of 800 students of Std. VIII from ten elementary schools in Lalgudi Educational District of Tamil Nadu State.

INSTRUMENTATION

The following tools were used for the present study:

1. PSK Reading Skill Test developed and standardized by the investigator for the purpose of pre testing and post testing.

2. Language Interest Inventory developed by the investigator.

3. Socio-Economic Status Scale.

4. Willingness Scale for Teachers.

5. Reaction Scale for Teachers.

DELIMITATIONS

1. Reading is a complex skill and the present investigation has taken into consideration only certain selected sub skills of the reading skill due to time and financial constraints.

2. The present investigation has been made with particular reference to the elementary schools in Lalgudi Educational District of Tamil Nadu State. This geographical limitation was necessary because of two reasons, the first being the vastness of the geographical area of the State of Tamil Nadu and the second being the time factor. However, data were collected from the different types of schools managed by the Government, Private and Harijan Welfare Board.

3. Though the elementary stage consists of three years i.e. standard VI to standard VIII, the focus of the present investigation is only on the standard VIII due to administrative, financial and time constraints. As standard VIII is the terminal stage for this elementary education leading to High School education, the present investigation has been made with particular reference to the standard VIII of the elementary stage.

LIMITATIONS

Though every care was taken by the investigator to study the effectiveness of Reciprocal Teaching as a technique of improving reading it is possible that a few components might have escaped the investigator's consideration in studying the multitude of components in this complex reading phenomenon.

The effect of discrepancies due to teacher variation is an unavoidable in such experimental studies. However, every effort has been taken by the investigator as much as possible to overcome this limitation by training the teachers who were involved in the experiment to ensure uniform standard.

ORGANISATION OF THE THESIS

The study is reported in five chapters. In the First Chapter, the problem has been introduced and the theoretical framework and the need for the study have been highlighted. In the Second Chapter, an account of some of the previous studies related to the present investigation, conducted in India and abroad are abstracted and the rationale of the present study is stated at the end of the chapter. The Third Chapter delineates the research procedure adopted for conducting the experiment. The Fourth Chapter presents a detailed report of the analysis and interpretation of data. The Fifth Chapter summarizes the findings and conclusions of the study, provides recommendations on the basis of the findings and also makes suggestions for further research.

2
Review of Related Literature

"Besides providing a foundation for the problem to be investigated, the literature review can demonstrate how the present study advances, refines, or revises what is already known".

Merriam (1988)

PURPOSE OF REVIEW

Conducting a literature review is a vital component of the research process. Familiarity with previous research and theory in the area of study can help in conceptualizing the problem, conducting the study and interpreting the findings.

"The value of any single study is derived as much from how it fits with and expands on previous work as from the study's intrinsic properties. If some studies seem more significant than others, it is because the piece of the puzzle they solve or the puzzle they introduce, is extremely important, not because they are solutions in and of themselves" (Cooper, 1984).

"An investigator who ignores prior research and theory chances pursuing a trivial problem, duplicating a study already done, or repeating others' mistakes. The goal of research - contributing to the knowledge base of the field may then never be realized" (Merriam, 1988).

The research studies reviewed in this chapter include closely related investigations, which have been carried out in India and abroad on various dimensions of the research problem selected by the investigator.

The review actually helped in the formulation of the problem, definition of objectives, selection of methodology, design of tools and interpretation of research results. However, they are presented in a chapter form in this thesis in a different sequence.

CONCEPTUAL REVIEW

Reading research is just a little more than a hundred years old. The earliest works were Emile Janal's paper on 'eye movement' published in 1879 and James McKeen Catell's papers on seeing and naming letters versus words published in 1886. It was not till the mid 1960s that any concrete attempt was made to conceptualize theories about the reading process. Studying reading from the psychological perspective added a new dimension to research in reading.

Both Smith and Goodman (1988) view listening and reading as parallel active processes. Smith believes that reading is only superficially different from the comprehension of speech. Goodman sees reading and listening as alternate forms of the same language process.

The reading process in its initial stage begins with the learning-to-read phase. This phase is usually divided into 3 phases - the cognitive phase, the mastering phase and the automaticity phase. The learner consciously concentrates on developing the skills of reading in the cognitive phase. Practice to master the skill is the key in the mastering phase. In the automaticity phase, the learner goes beyond the mastery phase and performs the skill without conscious effort. Though the three phases are not clearly distinguishable into watertight compartments, they may overlap each other. A reader becomes a fluent reader when he reaches the automaticity phase so that he decodes print and processes meaning simultaneously without any effort and without being aware of it. Reading, thus becomes a naturally free flowing process from one point to the next.

Smith and Goodman (1988) suggest that reading ability depends on the reader's use of linguistic and non-linguistic information to make predictions about what is coming next. Goodman calls this "a willingness to take part in the psycho linguistic guessing game" while Smith calls this "a readiness to make guesses". Whether the employment of prediction is good and whether it is the only way all readers read is arguable. Mostly, what is 'next' in 'predicting what comes next' is debatable. It has been variously defined as sentence, paragraph and chapter. Also, no definite method for developing the prediction technique in reading has been developed yet. The difficulty lies in taking into account several acceptable answers for a given idea to be predicted in the reading process.

Is the knowledge of functioning of language essential for students to learn? This is the question teachers encounter while acquainting learners with the process of reading. Linguistic awareness and reading have a symbiotic effect on each other so that being linguistically aware enhances reading comprehension and the process of reading helps in becoming more linguistically aware.

It is this awareness that makes the distinction between a beginner and a fluent reader. A beginner concentrates more on decoding the language in order to extract meaning from the text. It is only with reading experience that comprehending while reading takes place naturally without paying conscious attention to the act of decoding.

There are many models to describe the process of decoding while reading a few with regard to the direction of information processing while decoding print to derive meaning. For instance, the Rumelhart model suggested that information processing is linear, that is, information is processed in a simple direction. But the reading process involves the interference of information in the higher stage with information in the lower stage. Thus the linear model failed to account for intermediary occurrences in reading. What was necessary was an interactive model, which permitted a merger of higher and lower stages of processing. Interactive models of reading appeared to provide a more accurate conceptualization of reading performance than strictly linear models. Interactive models were also in a better position to explain the difference in the use of linguistic data between good and poor readers.

After looking at decoding from the view of the direction of information processing, it becomes necessary to consider the psycholinguistic process involved in decoding. This was an area of controversy centering on the pertinent question whether in fluent readers, comprehension was dependent on the phonological process or whether it depended directly on visual input. Greg Brooks (1984) argued that they can be collectively called 'single route' theories as he assumed that only one of the two routes existed. Brooks suggested a third and logical possibility where "both routes exist and are active, either at different levels of fluency of the reader, or at different levels of difficulty of the text, or at different stages between first learning to read and becoming fluent". He called it the "parallel" model, which has been diagrammatically represented below.

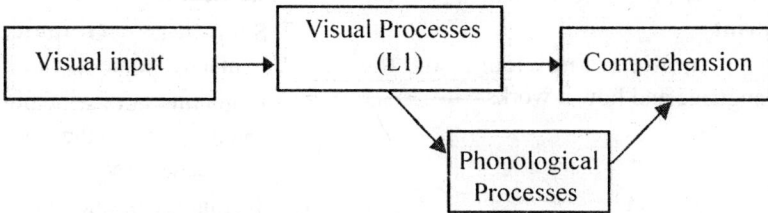

Fig 2.1: Brooks' Parallel Model Theory of Reading (1984)

According to the parallel model, while reading, visual processing and phonological processing take place simultaneously as the reader comprehends. The parallel model puts the debate of the single route theories to rest.

In decoding, it can be seen that meaning and code are complementary to each other. The cognitive clarity theory proposed by Downing (1982) claims to give equal weightage to both and lays emphasis on the cognitive phase of learner understanding. The creators of the writing system view language as a visual code whose linguistic awareness includes the awareness of the communicative function of language and certain features of spoken language. On the part of the readers, the process of learning to read is a rediscovery of the functions and coding rules of the writing system. This rediscovery depends on the readers' linguistic awareness. It is the same linguistic awareness to which the creators of the writing system had access. Children while learning to read, begin with a cognitive confusion about the purposes and technical aspects of language but gradually work themselves out of confusion into clarity.This alternate cycle of confusion and clarity continues throughout the later stages of reading as learners come across new sub-skills adding to their overall repertory of the reading skill.

On comparing Downing's (1982) cognitive clarity theory with Goodman's (1988) reading theory, it may be observed that both of them lay stress on linguistic awareness. Downing's hypothesis of confusion and clarification is analogous to Goodman's prediction and confirmation.

Reading comprehension is governed not only by the reader's ability to decode print and derive meaning from it but more importantly by his knowledge of the language and his experience of the world. This is what the reader brings to the print. Building on the insights provided by Goodman (1988), the reading process has been illustrated as follows.

What the Reader brings to the Print	**The Reading Process**
Implicit knowledge of the language and how it works	1. Sampling Graphic, Syntactic, semantic clues,
	2. Predicting both structure and meaning on the basis of selected areas.
	3. Testing the prediction.
	4. Either confirming the prediction or correcting if
Experience of the world	necessary.

Reading Process

What the reader brings to the print is due to his prior knowledge of the language and of the world. This prior knowledge that the reader brings to the text is well explained in the schema theories of comprehension. The schema is a high level domain-specific cognitive structure which can be viewed as "a framework of knowledge operating in a super ordinate fashion to interpret information". The schema is equivalent to other building blocks of knowledge i.e. "schemata", "scripts" and "macro structures". Research based on schema theory has shown that reading comprehension varies from one schema to another i.e. one domain of knowledge to another.

It is interesting to note that the schema theory gains significance because of its applicability to the conceptual network of knowledge/ information in Artificial Intelligence studies where the schema can be directly equated with 'frames' and 'scripts'. Frames are data structures of knowledge representation in Artificial Intelligence. Scripts are analogous to frames but are more specialized to deal with even sequences. Frames and 'scripts' in reading theory is the existing assumptions or background knowledge in language. Every act of comprehension involves one's knowledge of the world as well. There is a three-way distinction within schemata. It can be divided into linguistic schemata, content schemata and formal schemata.

◈   Linguistic schemata - reader's prior linguistic knowledge

◈   Content schemata - reader's prior background knowledge of the content area of the text.

◈   Formal schemata - reader's prior knowledge of the rhetorical structure.

The concept of schema is domain-specific. It is a representation of a particular aspect of knowledge containing slots to which values can be assigned. Combinations of schema form conceptual networks to characterize the nature of knowledge. The interpretation of a text depends on the relationship between the existing schema and the input information. This involves a top-down search or a bottom-up search. A top-down search is a concept-driven search for values, which 'fit', i.e., which meet the variable constraints of a knowledge frame that will accommodate particular values. The interpretation of the text involves a convergence of both the searches besides using knowledge in relevant frames. During the process either new schema are created or the existing schema are modified. Thus "interpretation is a function of the high-level schemata employed during comprehension and recall, as well as the corresponding fit between the selected schemata and information to be learned and remembered". The processing of information using frames in Expert Systems in Artificial Intelligence is done on similar lines using the knowledge base programs for reading comprehension. Frames can be used as the equivalent of schemata as the building blocks of cognition. Here, prior knowledge has a great role to play.

So, it can be concluded that a good reader must be linguistically aware and he must be able to use his linguistic awareness and his knowledge of the world to decode print and derive meaning. The act of decoding may be in the form of prediction, confirmation and correction or rejection of the prediction.

Reading Strategies

The process or reading consists of the readers' application of certain reading strategies to drive meaning from print. Studies have shown that the reading process was the same for everyone and that the use of the three curing systems for reading namely graphophonic, syntactic and semantic was universal. Despite the universality, the discrepancy in the proficiency level among readers may be attributed to the varying efficiency with which readers carry out the reading process. The differing levels of reading efficiency may be due to the differing reading strategies that readers employ.

The more the reader reviews the reading process, the greater is the probability of coming up with an "optimal strategy for effective interaction". A general and common reading strategy that all readers use irrespective of the language in which they read can be described as follows.

The reader scans the words to see whether his or her prediction matches the meaning of the words. If they do, there is closure and the reader supplies the meaning, generating comparing and scanning process to the next part of the text. When there is mismatch in the expected meaning and the meaning found in the text, the process of reading falters. The reader at this stage may come up with a strategy and search again, reading for revised meaning. Otherwise, the reader might give up attaching meaning to the text.

In the use of reading strategies, the ability to use various types of textual constraints is related to competence level in the language. The competence level depends on the readers' metacognitive knowledge i.e., "the stable, expressible although sometimes incorrect knowledge that learners have acquired about language learning process. Learners use their intuition to formulate their own theories about the reading process basing it on their knowledge about their own learning abilities. Prior knowledge includes not only the learner's knowledge of language and the world as Goodman (1988) has proposed but the knowledge about their own learning competence as well. Clear distinctions have been made between 'poor' and 'good' reading strategies. The less competent readers used poor strategies like reproducing exactly the orthographic features of text words, relying on the bottom-up strategies for processing information while the more proficient readers employed both graphic and contextual clues, besides using non-textual information or higher order schemata.

The gap between poor and good reading strategies can be bridged with reading practice and guidance form the teacher. Accepting that the reader uses the strategies of prediction, confirmation and correction as he develops his reading skill with experience, the role of the teacher's instructions are of paramount importance in the initial stages to provide practice in the learning-to-read process. The teacher's instruction must enable the reader to read according to sense groups rather than read word by word. The strategies for teaching should aim at the acquisition of rapid reading and the ability to adjust the speed according to the text and purpose. Besides being able to skim for the main idea and scan for specific kinds of information, reading critically should also be encouraged. Gradually the poor reader is bound to use his own intuition and reach the high proficiency level in reading. The cause of poor reading is lack of reading practice. With a persevering attitude and extensive reading practice any reader can improve his linguistic awareness. Practice can also bring about change in the attitude to reading. Findings have shown that unpractised readers differed primarily from practised readers in their ability to use the linguistic clues in the large context to determine meaning. They found it especially difficult to deduce word meaning from context, to understand lexical cohesion and to understand the meaning relationships between sentences. Students can be trained to become more aware of language and understand the clues it provides to derive meaning.

Before being able to achieve the higher order skills of reading like problem solving, reasoning to make inferences not explicitly stated in the text, understanding cause-effect relationships etc., teaching of certain important strategies are essential at the secondary school level. Learners are expected to know and use strategies for cognitive learning. Every reading sub-skill demands the use of certain strategies.

❖ Use own language or second language to infer meaning.

❖ Use knowledge about world, culture and communication process to infer meaning or predict outcomes.

❖ Relate new information to physical actions.

❖ Distinguish relevant from irrelevant clues for determining meaning.

Similarly, deductive reasoning demands the following strategies.

❖ Infer grammatical rules or word formation by analogy.

❖ Look for regularities and exception in grammar, word formation and phonology style.

❖ Synthesized understanding of language system.

❖ Use schema to grasp overall semantic intention.

In a classroom, two kinds of reading strategies are used -strategies that learners use based on their metacognitive knowledge and strategies that teachers use for training students. Two important pre-reading teaching strategies that teachers employ in classroom teaching to promote proficiently in reading are SQ3R and advance organizers.

SQ3R as a Pre-Reading Strategy

SQ3R is a much venerated pre-reading strategy in which 'S' stands for 'Survey' and involves glancing over the headings to find out the main points to be discussed 'Q' stands for 'Question' and requires Reading,

Reciting and Reviewing. Searching for answer in the questions is done by reading. Reciting involves thinking over the answer the reader has arrived at by looking away from the text. The review is done by reconstructing the whole process in the mind by once again going through the survey. As it involves multiple strategies it makes a very demanding task on the reader. SQ3R technique can be introduced late to students at high school level to ensure better independent application of the technique by mature students. Mastering the SQ3R technique banks heavily on students' ability to use cues in the text from beginning to end. This is considered a disadvantage for three reasons.

1. As the students have to rely solely on the cues in the text, the search becomes very text-based. It does not encourage the student to use his prior knowledge or develop background knowledge for reading.

2. If headings and subheadings are not logically organized to reflect key concepts in the text, then the purpose of survey and question may be defeated.

3. The students may be influenced by the author's perspective, as they have to rely only on the cues in the text and may not develop alternate perspectives of a topic.

It cannot be claimed that because the survey requires searching for cues in the text, background knowledge of the reader cannot be developed. Though it must be agreed that poorly selected heading can impede the development of the survey and question techniques in reading, the usefulness of survey and questioning concept itself cannot be denied. That the author's perspective will affect the development of critical reading is a weak argument.

Advance Organizer as a pre-Reading Strategy

Advance organizer is another pre-reading/pre-instructional strategy. Its purpose is to "assist the reader in mastery of forthcoming concepts by providing a framework of scaffolding prior to the reading assignment". To put it simply the meaningful learning of a reader is dependent upon the reliability of the reader's established cognitive structure to new concepts. The organizer is read in advance of the text to be learnt. This provides the reader with a conceptual framework which.

(a) gives him a general overview of the major detailed material in advance of his actual confrontation with it and

(b) also provides organizing elements that are inclusive of and take into account most relevantly and efficiently the particular content contained in the material.

Organizers vary for different pre-reading tasks. They depend on the nature of the learning material, the reader's age and the reader's prior familiarity with the given learning material. Hence it is difficult to be precise about the organizer construction.

Other pre-reading strategies teachers use in liassroom vary from group discussions to pretests as forms of assessment. For example, before embarking on the task of reading of a particular lesson, the teacher can organize a group discussion based on the theme of the lesson. Learner participation though group discussion and differing points of view by learners during the discussion can enrich the reading task that is to follow.

In order to gauge the reader's competence level, the teacher can also use pretests for assessment. They can be simultaneously used to record the learner's performance over a period of time and to search for common errors that a group of learners may make.

The principal aim of using reading strategies is to comprehend the text. When students read, their use of reading strategies depends on

◈ their prior knowledge

◈ the nature of the reading task

◈ the result the teacher expects from the students

◈ the result the students expect from the reading task

Effective reading strategies can be arrived at by the learners' reading practice and by training given by the teacher in the classroom.

"Reading is the process by which the child can, on the run, extract a sequence of cues from printed texts and relate these one to another, so that he understands the precise message of the text. The child continues to gain in this skill throughout his entire education, interpreting statements of ever increasing complexity" (M.M.Clay, 1972).

Psychologists believe that reading is a human behaviour and is to be considered a skill. In the educational context, 'reading skills' is the term used often because skills in curriculum and instruction courses usually refer to mental or motor activities that are taught as part of the curriculum. In psychology, in contrast, the term skill is a label for a specific category of behaviour. There are many activities of reading that contribute to the behaviour of reading as a whole.

The hypothesis about the skill of reading is that is comprises a number of sub-skills, which can be differential and described. Therefore it is believed that it can be taught and tested. Brown and Hirst (1983) argue that this is an incorrect notion and offer two alternative theories - a "discrete skills approach" and a "holistic integrated approach". The discrete skills approach sees reading as the summation of micro-skills which can be taught and tested. The holistic integrated approach sees reading as an interaction between reader and text which cannot be usefully analyzed into 'x' number of skills without totally distorting what actually goes on in the reading act. The sum of the parts is greater than the whole when we divide the interaction between the reader and the text into 'x' number of skills. The discrete skills approach is more practical and adds support to the traditional teaching, followed over the years in classrooms, that the reading processes can be divided into so many skills and can be taught in the classroom situation.

The different theories proposed by cognitive scientists are varied in their approach and no single principle acceptable to all exists. There are as many terms as there are theorists willing to classify reading skills. The earliest classification or reading skills into intensive reading and extensive reading was done by Palmer(1920). Reading may also be classified into reading interpretation and fluent reading etc.

Brumfit (1980) provides a more holistic classification by dividing reading into a skills and non-skills process. He divides reading skills into the mechanical skills, the intellectual skills and the non-skills study according to the ability to respond to language beyond plain statement (Fig.2.2). The mechanical skills can be divided into the ability to derive concepts from printed or written symbols, ability to read fast, ability to vary speed in accordance with reading aims and the ability to read aloud so as to achieve meaningful communication with one's listeners.

The intellectual skills comprise reading for exact information, reading for implied meaning, reading for gist, reading for required information and projective reading. The ability to read fast and the ability to vary speed according to the reading purpose is related to intellectual skills.

The non-skills study or the ability to respond to language beyond plain statement includes sensitivity to humour, irony, emotive language, the writer's philosophy, the writer's aims and sympathies and response leading to studies of a more literary nature. Reading for meaning and 'projective' reading are related to the non-skills study.

THE MECHANICAL SKILL

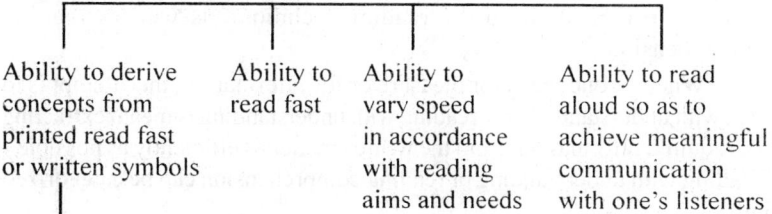

Ability to derive concepts from printed read fast or written symbols	Ability to read fast	Ability to vary speed in accordance with reading aims and needs	Ability to read aloud so as to achieve meaningful communication with one's listeners

THE INTELLECTUAL SKILLS

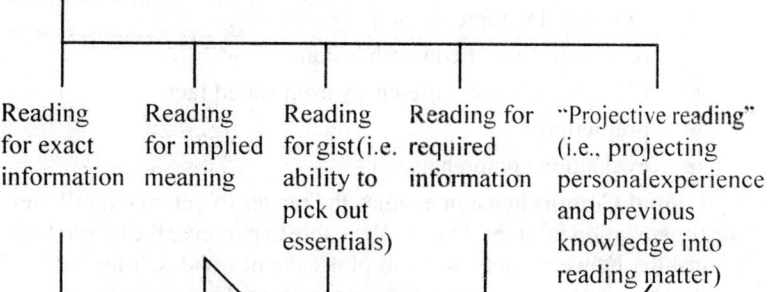

Reading for exact information	Reading for implied meaning	Reading for gist (i.e. ability to pick out essentials)	Reading for required information	"Projective reading" (i.e., projecting personal experience and previous knowledge into reading matter)

NON -SKILLS STUDY

Ability to respond to language beyond plain statement

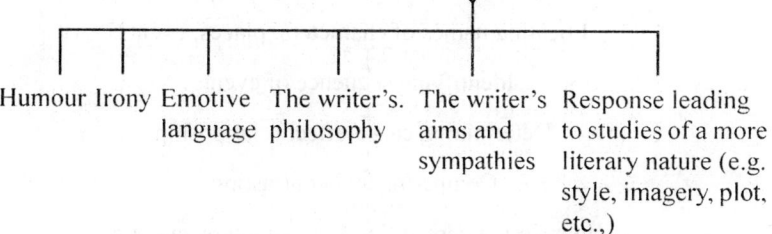

Humour	Irony	Emotive language	The writer's. philosophy	The writer's aims and sympathies	Response leading to studies of a more literary nature (e.g. style, imagery, plot, etc.,)

Fig 2.2 : Classification of Reading Skills

Independent of the plethora of terms that can be attributed to reading skills, the process of reading involves a combination of reading techniques and reading comprehension. A skilled reader anticipates on the basis of his previous experience, responds automatically by automation and analyses and feedback that he gets from perceptual signals. Reading skills as a whole contribute to the reading technique as well as reading comprehension.

Whether one reads for pleasure or for information, the attempt is to read with understanding. By reading with understanding is meant extracting the required information 'from the written matter as efficiently as possible'. Reading with understanding or reading comprehension can be categorized into

- ❖ global comprehension
- ❖ local comprehension
- ❖ referential comprehension
- ❖ reorganization of comprehension
- ❖ the ability to draw inferences from stated facts
- ❖ prediction
- ❖ evaluation comprehension

Global Comprehension enables the reader to get an overall view of the organization in a text. The reader is able to perceive the hierarchical relationships between plots and sub-plots, themes and sub-themes and understand their logical organization into paragraphs.

Local Comprehension is the ability to locally identify and understand isolated pieces information like facts or clues. This leads to the natural concomitant of making inferences from these facts. Local comprehension can be graded from locating the names of characters, places, events etc., to comprehend the main theme of the text.

LOCAL COMPREHENSION

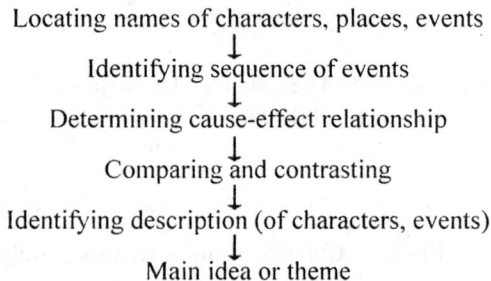

Locating names of characters, places, events
↓
Identifying sequence of events
↓
Determining cause-effect relationship
↓
Comparing and contrasting
↓
Identifying description (of characters, events)
↓
Main idea or theme

Referential Comprehension is the ability to recover specific information by referring to the different parts of the text. Referential comprehension varies from single factual comprehension which requires the reader to pack out information directly from a single place in the text, to a more complex referential comprehension which requires locating and recovering information in bits dispersed over the full length of the text. The reader will have to link bits of information occurring in different parts of the text to answer a question like 'give a list of reasons for x'.

Reorganization of Information differs from the higher form of referential comprehension as it requires the learner to rearrange or reorganize information that may not have been presented in a manner convenient to understand or easy to remember. The reader can reorganize information in the text by making notes for easier understanding. These notes can be in the form of classifying, categorizing and simultaneously summarizing.

Inferential Comprehension is the ability to draw inference from stated facts. Things not stated explicitly can be summarized by filling the gaps for information. Inferential comprehension is a higher level comprehension than the factual or referential comprehension as it involves reasoning ability. A commonly held view among language teachers is that, the teaching of reasoning abilities does not come under the domain of language teaching. It is not advisable to overlook the importance of responding to linguistic stimulus. Readers should be sensitive to linguistic stimuli and always keep their eyes open for clues.

Prediction is the ability to predict what is likely to follow on the basis of what has been read. Inferential comprehension and organization of information play an important role in the skill of predicting, as the reader has to look for clues as well as comprehend the logical organization of information.

Evaluation Comprehension is the ability to judge the content of the text from the point of view of credibility, acceptability, authorial prejudices, narrative style and literary criticism. The skill of evaluation comprehension improves with reading experience.

Methods of Teaching Reading

It is a common view that the teaching of reading ranks uppermost in the language teaching priorities.

Early methods of the teaching of reading concentrated more on decoding print. The Alphabetic Method laid stress on letter recognition. The Phonic Method attempted recognition of sounds. The Whole Word Method concentrated on the shape of the word. The Sentence Method aimed at understanding the sentence as a whole. The Kinesthetic Method taught reading through touch. The Look-Say Method required the combination of visual and oral skills. The Phonic Word Method was a combination of the Phonic and Look-Say Method and the linguistic approach suggested a holistic approach to the teaching of reading.

It is essential to decode print to understand the text but decoding is only one half of the reading process. The major flaw in all these methods was that they concentrated only on decoding print while reading and gave no importance to the other half of the reading process-deriving meaning and understanding.

Reading involves decoding the meaning and not decoding the sound. That the technique of reading was only one half of the reading process was confirmed when teaching methods were divided into the code emphasis and meaning emphasis thereby finding a clear cut division in the attitude of teachers and researchers to give more importance to either teaching children the meaningful communication aspect of the text or the technical aspects of reading.

The ultimate goal of the method employed for teaching reading should be to enable the learner to read independently, rapidly and with understanding.

The principal feature of the Reading Method is that it restricts the goals of language teaching to training in reading comprehension. Stern (1984) cites West (1926) and Bond (1953) as providing contemporary arguments for the approach. West (1926) produced a series of course books, which he called New Method Readers. Coleman (1929) believed while teaching in American high schools that reading should take precedence over other skills. Bond (1953) developed a reading method at Chicago University for college language courses. The Reading Method came for criticism in America, when during the Second World War, speaking English gained priority over reading. Stern states that the most important technique advocated in this method was vocabulary control and the difference between intensive reading and extensive reading. Stern affirms that "that reading method grew out of practical education considerations, not from a shift in linguistic or psychological theory". The byproducts of the reading method were

◈   deriving language learning techniques for specific purposes.

◈   applying vocabulary control for better grading of texts.

◈   creation of graded readers.

◈   the introduction of rapid reading techniques because of the application of vocabulary control .

RESEARCH REVIEW

Reading is a basic tool for achieving proficiency in all school subjects. The success of any student in the school is largely dependent on the extent to which his reading skills have been developed.

Reading in its sociological, psychological and pedagogical aspects has for over a century been the most persistently investigated of the receptive processes of communication. Historically considered, the development of research in reading closely mirrors that of educational research in general and of educational psychology in particular.

Research in the field of reading was first done in the laboratories of Europe. Psychologists studied the nature of reading act and the way in which words are perceived and recognised.

In 1930s, the evolution movement under the leadership of Tyler began to make itself felt as attempts to define the objectives of reading instruction in behavioral terms. By the year 1940, factorial analysis techniques were being used to describe more precisely the components of reading comprehension.

Research work undertaken in subsequent years was better controlled, more sophisticated and well designed. Sensitive instruments like Opthalmograph, Reading Accelerator, Reading Board, Metronoscope, the push card method etc., were used in those investigations.

Studies conducted on reading in foreign countries are in different perspectives as reading habits, reading readiness, reading speed and comprehension, reading interest and methods of teaching reading. In India, attention of researchers and educationists have been directed to this field and a few studies have been reported by the investigators in the language of Marathi, Gujarati, Hindi, and Kannada.

Reading theories of Schema (the knowledge that is organised and stored in the reader's mind is called schema or Schemata) of 1970's were revised by Anderson and Pearson (1984); Spiro, Coulson, Feltovich and Anderson (1980); Spiro, Vispoel, Shritz, Samara Pungavis, and Borger, (1987); Rosenblatt (1978, 1983) transactional views of the relationship between the reader and writer; Vygosky (1981) and Bakhtin (1981) provided ammunition for socially based views of cognition, learning and development and Sulzby and Teale (1991) review of emergent literacy were some of the important studies on reading.

Rajagopalan (1981) studied the relationship of selected variables to reading comprehension in English and found that pupils experienced greater difficulty in recognizing the meanings of words than in dealing with sentence forms and continuous pieces of writing.

Subramaniam (1981) studied the correlates of reading achievement and found that reading achievement in Telugu was positively related to the general mental ability, visual ability and speech habits of children. He studied the variables viz., reading habits, family income, education of the parents, caste, encouragement of the parents, time spent on reading activities in their home in relation to reading achievement and found that they were highly positively related.

Development of reader resources in relation to text begins when parents or teachers start to read to children, sometimes as early as age three. The children learn that reading is an enjoyable and worthwhile activity and that stories have certain characteristics. Initially they learn that stories have a beginning, middle, and end, and the characters in them try solve a problem in one or more ways and eventually are successful or else give up. Thus preschoolers begin to acquire the knowledge structures of story grammar and use them to guide their listening and retrieval of information from memory (Slinger, 1982).

Picture-story method, language experience approach (Singer, 1982); individualized reading, and basal reader (Singer, 1984) are the few new approaches suggested for the pupils in the research discovery.

Gentle, Lance (1983) studied the importance in sports in relation to reading and writing activities and found that sports-oriented students may use their experience directly and become active participants in the reading process.

Epstein, Joyce (1984) and Peryon (1985) found that parent involvement made greater gains in reading achievement than did other students.

Pandolfo, Jidith Martin (1985) studied how background knowledge of the content of text affects reading comprehension and the role it plays in the diagnosis and instruction of reading comprehension skills for linguistically/culturally diverse students may be demonstrated through schema theory. Since a schema represents what is believed to be generally true about a class of things, events, or situation, an individual's concepts about the world can also be discussed in terms of schema theory. Studies have provided evidence that background knowledge is important in reading comprehension, especially for linguistically/culturally diverse students. Furthermore, the linguistic and cultural experiences of an individual play a crucial role in the development of the schematic knowledge style. The closer the match between the content schema used in writing the text and the schema chosen by the reader to interpret the test, the better the level of comprehension. Linguistically/culturally diverse students can be adversely affected in their reading assessment and instruction by materials for which they lack the appropriate background knowledge. Responsible educators must be aware of the linguistic and cultural diversity of their students, and should provide appropriate materials and methods.

Peryon (1985) edited 11 papers presented on the general theme, "Factors other than teaching that influence reading achievement". The following topics are covered: (1) The relationship between culture and reading achievement, (2) The influence of language on reading, (3) Levels of cultural knowledge and self-esteem of intermediate grade participants in a Philippine heritage curriculum, (4) Effects of administrative leadership on reading achievement, (5) Proximodistal direction in the selection of reading materials, (6) Survival reading skills, (7) The relationship between intelligence and reading achievement, (8) Aspects of self-concept as related to thee reading process, (9) Parents do make a difference, (10) The use and effectiveness of computers in reading instruction, and (11) Identification of a dyslexic, with some contributing factors.

Johnston Rhona et al., (1987) studied the influence of phonology on good and poor readers and found that both type of readers can generate phonological codes from print and use to make judgements about the meaningfulness of sentences.

Spiro et al., (1987, 1988) argued that the schema model of comprehension so dominant in the decade from 1975 to 1985 risks over simplification of comprehension and learning by implying that schema have a fixed, static character. They argued for the need to expand schema theory to account for the dynamic nature of comprehension and learning, especially in domains of knowledge, that have an ill-structured character, that is, where the category distracts are fuzzy and the operational rules have numerous exceptions.

Vocabulary development in any subject can proceed by asking students to reveal any vocabulary framework that they already have. These known words may help them associate meaning with new vocabulary. In that way, definitions and the particular meaning within a given sentence have a context (Smith, 1988).

With respect to advances in knowledge about word identification Foss (1988) and Stanovich (1991) contributed over the role of context in word identification. Smith and Goodman (Encyclopedia of Educational Research, 1992) have argued that good readers use contextual information to reduce the need for extensive letter-by-letter processing in order to achieve word identification and lexical access.

Barton and Calfer (1989) suggest using a vocabulary matrix to establish the dimensions of the subject. The power of any vocabulary matrix lies in its image of connected ideas, in its process of discovering context for a new word, and in its visual reminder of gaps in our understanding.

Mc Ghee, Paul et al., (1990) found that intersection of classes and divergent thinking skills contributed to metaphor and humorous comprehension.

Dash (1991) studied the cognitive and speech related processes in relation to reading efficiency and IQ. Dave (1992) investigated on reading comprehension of the pupils in Gujarati. Dave et al., (1988), Deb and Hirdaipal (1990) and Dave (1991) studied on pupils achievement.

Masterson et al., (1992) in "Beginning Reading with Phonology" examined processes involved in reading aloud and printed word comprehension of 44 children. Students were in 2nd year of reading instruction and read pairs of regular and irregular words in task one and regularly spelled homophones in task two. Use of assembled phonology was evident in students' reading aloud responses, and proficiency in its use was related to reading ability. Printed-word comprehension appeared to involve prior retrieval of a phonological code for less frequent words. Similarities between the processing systems for reading used by these students and by skilled readers were highlighted.

Ong, Jin et al., (1992) examined the reliability of the amplitude of the return-sweep velocity in reading. Eye movements of 26 male college student were recorded, once without spectacle corrections and then with piano lenses on a trial frame. Reliability of the amplitude of the return-sweep velocity on these two trials was moderately high, meaning that both the desirable as well as the undesirable reading habits are probably deeply rooted by college. Reading remediation or improvement training should be performed at much earlier stages to be effective.

Masson, Michael (1993) reported that explored fluent reading comprehension in 6 experiments involving sentences presented in normal and inverted typography. 226 college students served as subjects. Sentences read in a test phase had been read earlier in exactly the same form or inversions that were created by altering the word order within sentence to create randomly ordered word strings or exchanging casually related clauses to form new meaningful sentences. Variation increased the time taken to read the test sentences and these effects were evident over retention intervals ranging from 1 day to 4 months. Results support an episodic view of the basis for reading fluency in which comprehension processes responsible for constructing and integrating proposition are automatically recruited and reapplied when a sentence is reread.

A 1996 survey published by the International Reading Association reported that 47 states and the District of Columbia required specific reading coursework in reading methods for pre-service middle school and high school teachers. The study concluded that unless the courses "encourage actual implementation of effective instructional techniques" there would be "little positive change" in the reading performance of U.S. content-area classrooms.

Janette Vaughn (1996) investigated the efficacy of two related interventions on the reading comprehension of seventh and eighth graders with learning disabilities who used English as a second language. As many as 26 students participated in reciprocal teaching for 15 days and then were randomly assigned for 12 days to 1 of 2 groups - Reciprocal Teaching with cooperative grouping (N=13) or reciprocal teaching with cross-age tutoring (N = 13). Though there was no statistically significant difference between groups, the students made significant progress in reading comprehension Analyses focused on understanding the performance of more and less successful students within group. Findings revealed that initial reading ability and oral language proficiency seemed related to gains in comprehension, that a greater range of students benefited from strategy instruction than would have been predicted on the basis of previous research, and that students in both groups continued to show improvement in comprehension when provided minimal adult support.

Karpaga Kumaravel and Gopalan (1997) conducted a survey of Reading Skills in Tamil among the High School students. The study included a Silent Reading Speed Test and Silent Reading Comprehension Test. Silent Reading Index was calculated to all the 170 students who participated in the study. The study concluded that (1) the male students' silent reading index was higher than that of the female students, (2) there was no significant difference in the performance in the silent reading test between the students with Tamil as the mother tongue and non-Tamil students.

RESEARCH STUDIES CONDUCTED IN 2002

Arnold, Karen Michele (2002) conducted a study entitled "The cognitive reading strategies and motivation to read resilient, average, and non-resilient fourth- and fifth-grade Latino English language learners". The study identified the cognitive reading strategies used by resilient, average, and non-resilient bilingual students while they are reading material in their second language (i.e., English). Differences by grade level were also explored. Additionally, aspects of the students' individual motivation to read are studied. Finally, information gathered about the students' cognitive reading strategies and motivation to read were analyzed in relation to achievement. The students participating in this study consisted of 99 fourth-grade and 97 fifth-grade resilient, average, and non-resilient bilingual Spanish-speaking students. These grade levels were targeted because they had been identified as a crucial transition period for all students. Overall results revealed that although the fourth- and fifth-grade resilient, average, and non-resilient students reported using a variety of reading strategies, the majority of those reported were weak or less sophisticated strategies. The resilient students had a significantly higher self-concept about reading as compared to non-resilient and average students. Suggestions for improving practice were made in the following areas; stronger reading strategy instruction, an emphasis on students' self-concept, and an increase in the quality and quantity of reading materials available at home and school. Future research needs to study resiliency in the field of reading, motivation to read factors that differentiate students by resiliency; and the impact of student testing as it is related to the reading instruction.

Archer, Steven Keith (2002) attempted to study the effects of social construction of meaning on the reading comprehension of middle school students. The purpose of this study was to investigate effects of social construction of meaning on reading comprehension of middle school students. Specifically, the study was designed to show that students significantly improved their memory of text content when afforded an opportunity to construct the meaning of printed text socially. The 76 sixth grade subjects from an urban school were assigned randomly to six different groups. Six teachers were trained to use three instructional approaches to teach three narrative reading selections. Each group received three types of instruction, each of which varied significantly on a social construction of meaning and arts based continuum. Treatment A involved the most social construction of meaning, with representations of story meaning by both the teacher and students. Treatment B involved less social construction of meaning, with representations of story meaning by the teacher only. Treatment C involved the least social construction of meaning, with traditional teacher-directed instruction. After each instructional session students wrote summaries of the story from memory. Summaries were evaluated to assess the number of idea units. A MANOVA analysis of the data supported the hypothesis that students willscore statistically significantly higher after receiving Treatment A than after Treatment B, and that students will score statistically significantly higher after receiving Treatment B than after Treatment C. The statistical significance favoring the hypothesis in each instance was at a .01 level. Results of the Teaching and Learning Beliefs Scale (George, 1999) indicated that the teachers in the study differed little in their beliefs regarding the value of social construction of meaning. These results indicated that the study results were not affected by teachers being heavily biased in favor of one of the types of instruction studied. This study indicated that students remembered narrative text much better when engaged in more social construction of meaning and when both the teacher and students engaged to a greater degree in representing the text with visual language construction and performance art. The implications are that more opportunities should be afforded to students to engage, and see their teachers engage, in socially constructing meaning of printed text.

Barber, Marsha Hairston (2002) conducted a study of first-grade students who were recommended for retention, were retained or promoted, and their later reading achievement. The study reviews the history of education in the United States and the birth of the retention/social promotion controversy. As the body of research grew over the last half of the 20th century, diametrically opposed results surfaced, putting retention and promotion proponents against each other. There was no research found in literature wherein the retention/social promotion issue had been studied in the Christian school setting. For this reason, the baseline data were collected. Research subjects were identified as students enrolled in Christian schools in the greater Dallas/Fort Worth area who struggled in first grade. Either the Association of Christian Schools International or the International Christian Accrediting Association accredited these Christian schools. Students were grouped according to whether the student was retained or promoted to second grade. Students' Total Reading Battery Stanford Achievement Test scores at the end of first grade and again at the end of third grade were compared to see which group showed the most improvement over this period of time. Results indicated that students who repeated first grade showed more improvement at the end of third grade based on Total Reading Battery scores of the Stanford Achievement Test. With these results in mind it is recommended that principals, teachers, and parents take into consideration the availability of retention as a solution to struggling in the early school years.

Bompadre, Constance Ellen (2002) studied the effectiveness of systematic reading programs on the achievement of students in grades K—2. Two groups of students in elementary school were studied to determine if two systematic reading programs, Project Read and Breakthrough to Literacy, increased student achievement as measured by the Test of Auditory Analysis Skills, the Basic Angling Skills Survey, the Yopp-Singer Test of Phoneme Segmentation, and a Qualitative Reading Inventory. Both groups of students were chosen from the same school district. The first group was instructed in Project Read in kindergarten through second grade and Breakthrough to Literacy in kindergarten and first grade. The second group of students were not instructed in either of these systematic reading programs; however, both School A and School B used the Houghton Mifflin series for the literature component of the language arts curriculum. Test scores on the survey instruments of phonemic awareness were obtained at the end of the students first grade year, and their comprehension was evaluated at the end of second grade. The data revealed that students who had direct, systematic instruction in phonemic awareness performed better in reading than those students who did not have that type of direct, systematic instruction. These results suggest that interaction with print combined with explicit attention to sound structure in spoken words supports children in learning to read.

Bouchard, Margaret Pray (2002) conducted an investigation of students' word knowledge as demonstrated by their reading and spelling errors. The research investigated four aspects of spelling as developmental word knowledge. First, the research examined the third graders' performances on a standardized spelling test and qualitative word knowledge inventory, and indicated that as students' spelling scores increased so did their word knowledge scores. Next, the study investigated the relationship of word knowledge development across four reading and spelling tasks. Using repeated-measures design, the third graders' performances and orthographic errors on an instructional-level, word knowledge inventory list were examined. An analysis of variance indicated that students' performances on the reading tasks were significantly better than their performances on the spelling tasks. A descriptive error analysis was employed to examine the developmental levels of the demonstrated errors across tasks and indicated that there was a significant task effect on the student's level of word knowledge. Further qualitative analysis of the reading and spelling errors of students revealed that the errors involved similar orthographic features across the tasks. Finally, the investigation explored the third grade teachers' rating of their students' spelling achievement and word knowledge. The data indicated that the ratings were significantly related to the students' actual performances in spelling achievement and word knowledge, but not adequate for instructional decisions. The findings suggested three pertinent considerations that need to be addressed in any analysis of reading and spelling errors. First, that the sample of reading and spelling errors needs to be large enough to be representative of their word knowledge development. Second, an error analysis that includes errors from different linguistic tasks, needs to consider the functional levels for each type of task. Further, the error analysis revealed that students use a combination of strategies, not only orthographic cues to both read and spell words.

Brink, Marilyn C.H (2002) carried out a study of family characteristics of first-grade students at-risk for retention as determined by the 'success for all reading roots eight-week assessment'. A large number of students were retained in first-grade each year at Sudduth Elementary School, Starkville, Mississippi, because they did not master reading levels necessary for promotion. The Success For All Reading Roots Eight-Week Assessment determined the reading level. A survey was sent to parents of 54 at-risk students; nineteen surveys were returned. Results were divided into two groups: promoted to second-grade or retained in first-grade according to their end-of-year reading level. The two groups were compared for differences in family involvement in the child's education. Data were analyzed using frequency counts and percentages. Previous studies demonstrated relationships among number of reading items available in the home, amount of parental involvement in their child's education, and academic success. The present study supported these findings: the more reading material in the home and the more positive parental involvement with the school, the more likely the child was to master first-grade reading.

Camacho, Martha Ariadna (2002) studied the effects of Waterford Early Reading Program on reading achievement of first-grade students. A field test was conducted on Waterford Early Reading Program (WERP) to evaluate its effect on reading achievement. The twelve-week field test was conducted in Harbor City, California. A class consisting of twenty first grade students, twelve boys and eight girls, was selected from Harbor

City Elementary School using a non-probability convenience sample. The entire sample of the field test was classified as English Language Learners (ELL). The numerical data gathered for the field test came from the Waterford Computer Adaptive Reading Test (WCART). The results indicate that after a twelve-week period, students' reading achievement significantly increased.

Campbell, Brenda Wright (2002) in her doctoral thesis entitled, "Genre Studies: Temporary homogeneous grouping to improve reading or merely another form of tracking?" attempted to study the effectiveness of a particular district-wide literacy strategy in its first year that focused on literacy to educate students identified as at-risk. Specifically, this study used data gathered from two measures of reading achievement, the Stanford Achievement Test (SAT) and the Stanford Diagnostic Reading Test (SDRT), to determine the impact that a special literacy block of classes, known as Genre Studies, had on the reading scores of 102 at risk children enrolled in a southern California secondary school. In addition to measuring the absolute success of these students, their relative success was also measured by comparing them with a matched sample of non-Genre Studies students from the previous year. Multiple regression analysis was also used to explain why some of the Genre Studies students gained more through the intervention than others. Results suggested that only a small percentage of the Genre Studies students (9%) became eligible for regular English classes as a result of the two-hour literacy block intervention. In fact, attendance, course credits, and students' need for modified curriculum all had a negative effect on the change in Genre Studies students' SDRT reading scores, whereas grade point average and Hispanic ethnicity had a positive effect on the change in the SDRT reading score. In addition, Hispanic students, and white females gained at least a year's growth in reading as a result of the intervention; Asian females gained almost a year's growth, African American females, Asian males, and white males showed a decline in their reading scores, and African American males showed no growth at all for the year. The analysis also revealed that students who took a regular, one-hour English class for a year did no worse than the Genre Studies students who participated in the two-hour literacy block class for a year. Thus, this study concluded that in at least one secondary school in southern California, the stratification of Genre Studies students into a homogeneous group was in essence, a de facto form of tracking.

Chaudhry, Naheed (2002) conducted a study entitled the "Use of comprehension strategies and reading in English as a second language by Pakistani immigrant children in New York City". The study was designed to explore the use of comprehension strategies on the reading comprehension of Culturally Familiar and Culturally Unfamiliar texts when they were presented to children from Pakistan who were engaged in English as a second language programs in the New York City Public School system. The participants were five female students and one male student who had been in the United States between one to three years and ranged in age from 11 to 13 years old. Each passage of approximately 250 words was read along with the Think Aloud (TA) technique. The major findings of the study were: 1) the students used more reading strategies with Culturally Familiar text than they did with Culturally Unfamiliar text; 2) they used similar explicit meaning strategies, such as restating what was read for the Culturally Familiar and Culturally Unfamiliar texts in approximately the same proportions; 3) they used more complex reading strategies with the Culturally Familiar text than they did with the Culturally Unfamiliar text. Conversely, the proportions of constructed meaning and evaluative meaning for the Culturally Familiar text were higher than for the Culturally Unfamiliar text; 4) constructed strategies were used quite differently between the two texts. For example, when reading the Culturally Familiar text, students were likely to add to the text from their own personal experience and provide examples of material presented in the text. In the Culturally Unfamiliar text, the most common constructed strategy was interpreting the text; in many cases misinterpreting the text; 5) students used constructed strategies at a ratio of nearly 2 to 1 for the Culturally Familiar text compared to the Culturally Unfamiliar text. They were also more likely to use a greater variety of constructed strategies, such as visualizing and making connections between different parts of the text; 6) evaluative strategies were used rarely; only seven such strategies were employed in the readings, mostly on the Culturally Familiar text; and 7) with the Culturally Familiar text, students were better able to recall details and elaborate on the passage than with the Culturally Unfamiliar text.

Durand, Barbara Angelia Cole (2002) attempted to study the effect of the Summer Reading Academy on the reading achievement of struggling third grade readers. The purpose of the study was to compare the effect of the Summer Reading Academy on the reading achievement of the third grade students who qualified and attended the Summer Reading Academy and the third grade students who qualified and did not attend the Summer Reading Academy. The Texas Assessment of Academic Skills was used as the measure of reading achievement. The participants for the study were 232 third grade students who scored below 70 per cent on the 2000 Texas

Assessment of Academic Skills and attended school in a large suburban Texas school district. These students were invited to attend the 2000 Summer Reading Academy. One hundred and sixteen of the students completed the Summer Reading Academy, which made up the Academy Group. One hundred sixteen of the students did not attend the Summer Reading Academy, which make up the Comparison Group. A quasi-experimental pretest-posttest control group research design was used to compare the progress made by Academy Group and progress made by the Comparison Group using the April 2000 and April 2001 Texas Assessment of Academic Skills reading sub-tests scores. The results reported indicated that there were no statistically significant differences ($p > .05$) between the Academy Group and the Comparison Group with regard to the six objectives measures by the reading section of the Texas Assessment of Academic Skills. Thus, the gains made by the Academy Group should not be attributed to their participation in the Summer Reading Academy. There is a need for more research, as high-stakes testing and reading education are on the rise nationwide. Teachers need more training in what to teach students who have been identified as struggling readers; and how to maintain increased reading levels when they are accomplished. Teachers also need better understanding of the test results and how to better target the reading needs of each individual student.

Marlow Ediger (2002), an authority on reading in his paper entitled "Pedagogical Consideration in Reading" discussed the pedagogical considerations in reading in terms of Teacher Directed Reading Pedagogy and Open-ended Programmes of Reading Instructions. He recommends the use of Basal Readers and Sustained Silent Reading (SSR) in teaching and learning of reading with an open-ended focus. In another article entitled "Pupil Decision Making in the Reading Curriculum", he discusses the role of pupil decision making in the reading curriculum in terms of sustained silent reading, personalised reading and the psychology of learning, and finally philosophy of reading instruction. He concluded that reading instruction can definitely make many contributions in order that pupils may achieve their objectives of reading, when decisions are made by the learners as to which library books to read sequentially.

RECIPROCAL TEACHING RESEARCH EXPERIENCES

Many research studies have been conducted to evolve a reading development strategy or set of strategies that would raise the reading levels of students. One such research was carried out in 1987 by Anne Marie

Palinscar, from Michigan State University and Anne Brown, from the University of Illinois and the outcome was the discovery of Reciprocal Teaching. The application of this Reciprocal Teaching strategy was experimented on urban students in Highland Park, Michigan during 1993-1995 and the success of the above experiment was reported by UNESCO-International Bureau of Education in 2001 in its *"Innodata Monographs -8 "*

King and Parent-Johnson (1990) reviewed the experiences they had in involving fifth grade teachers in studying Reciprocal Teaching and found that when teachers consistently and clearly modeled all four strategies, students monitored their comprehension and gained deeper insight into text concepts.

The research pool concerned with Reciprocal Teaching has likewise increased significantly. Practitioners have a wealth of information available to them through home pages and web sites, specialized bibliographies, descriptions of the process and the modifications tried in trials, and training materials. Examples of these include a training programme sponsored by the Florida Department of Education in which training materials were developed to acquaint middle school teachers in eight schools with Reciprocal Teaching. Patti's Electronic Classroom provides descriptive information on Reciprocal Teaching and provides training aids such as cards and scripts. A theory on practice monograph describes Reciprocal Teaching and provides practitioners with answers to the most commonly asked questions about the approach.

Kelly et al., (1994) assessed the effects of Reciprocal Teaching on the comprehension of poor readers and found significant improvement in comprehension that was maintained after an eight-week follow-up. A replication study conducted by Alfassi (1998), which investigated the effects of strategy instruction, was superior to traditional reading comprehension and concluded that the effects of strategy instruction was superior to traditional reading methods in fostering reading comprehension as measured by standardized reading tests.

The North Central Regional Educational Laboratory, an educational resource laboratory, has a website that explains Reciprocal Teaching and summarizes the research from which it comes. The University of Washington posts a Reciprocal Teaching Home Page that reviews the research and concludes that the technique is effective. In fact, an Internet search Reciprocal Teaching resources received 122,000 sites. This increase signals wide-ranging interest in Reciprocal Teaching.

Further, Reciprocal Teaching has aroused international interest as well. An example includes 'the European Union: Challenges to integration', which integrates both higher-order thinking skills and Reciprocal Teaching. In Canada, Hewitt (1995) published a review of Reciprocal Teaching that concludes that the technique is attractive for its simplicity of form and success in realizing its goals.

INSIGHTS FROM THE REVIEW AND RATIONALE OF THE PRESENT STUDY

(1) Studies abstracted in the six surveys of research in Education (1974, 1979, 1986, 1991, 1996 and 2000) revealed that no study has been conducted in India to test the effectiveness of Reciprocal Teaching Technique for improving reading at the elementary level. In this sense, the present study is unique against the series of studies covered in this review.

(2) From the review of literature, the investigator understands that a substantial body of empirical studies done abroad in countries like U.S.A. and Canada finds that Reciprocal Teaching has significant advantages as a reading improvement strategy. However, in the Indian context, the potentiality of Reciprocal Teaching as a reading improvement strategy needs to be tested against empirical data of actual research findings.

(3) A look back into all the researchers done with regard to Reciprocal Teaching brought out the gaps and overlaps and helped the investigator in identifying the research gap. The review presents a picture of a bunch of studies in reading and not even a single study in India on Reciprocal Teaching. Hence, the investigator took a planned effort to fill this research gap.

(4) The above studies reviewed are mainly helpful in developing the method and procedure adopted in the present study. A notable feature is that in the extensive literature reviewed in the present study, there has been no recorded evidence of any research work having been carried out on Reciprocal Teaching as a Technique for Improving Reading Skill at the Elementary Level. It is in this context that the present study becomes important and essential as endorsed by the specific concerns of earlier researchers both in its aims of the study and its procedures.

3
Methodology of the Study

"Research may be defined as the systematic and objective analysis and recording of controlled observations that may lead to the development of generalizations, principles or theories, resulting in prediction and possibly ultimate control of events."

Best, John W, 1986

SELECTION OF APPROPRIATE RESEARCH PROCEDURE

The heartthrob of any research activity is the research procedure adopted by the investigator. The method used in the study is dictated by the nature of the problem and the type of data required for answering the questions relating to the problem. An inappropriate procedure can only lead to unsatisfactory results and disillusionment. After selecting the proolem, framing the objectives and reviewing the related literature, the next important step in research is to explain the details of the various steps followed in the research design.

The previous two chapters were devoted to presenting the significance of the problem under investigation and for reviewing the related literature. In this chapter, the research procedure adopted for the study undertaken is described in detail.

Any research study involves the elements of observation, description, and analysis of what happens under certain circumstances. Best and Kahn (1989) evolved a simple three point analysis to classify educational research, as given in the next page.

Historical Research: It describes 'What was?' The process involves investigating, recording, analyzing, and interpreting the events of the past for the purpose of discovering relationships. The generalizations are helpful in understanding the past and the present, and to a very limited extent, in anticipating the future.

Descriptive Research: It describes 'What is?' The process involves describing, recording, analyzing, and interpreting conditions that exist. It involves some type of comparison or contrast and attempts to discover relationships between existing non-manipulated variables.

Experimental Research: It describes 'What will be?'. The process involves deliberate manipulation of certain variables with certain others being suppressed. The focus is on establishment of variable relationships.

The method of research pursued for this study is an appropriate blend of Experimental Method and Descriptive Method and Quantitative and Qualitative approaches. The present study is descriptive because an attempt has been made to find out the willingness and reaction of teachers and the willingness of students towards Reciprocal Teaching using normative survey willingness and reaction scales. The study is experimental to the extent that an attempt has been made to improve the Reading Skill by providing an experimental treatment namely Reciprocal Teaching.

METHODS OF COLLECTING THE DATA

Some of the major distinctions between quantitative and qualitative research paradigms discussed by Bogdan and Birklen (1982), Reichard and Collk (1979), Guba (1978), Owen (1982), and Leininger (1985) that are summarized and tabulated by Merriam (1988) are shown in Table 3.1 and Fig. 3.1

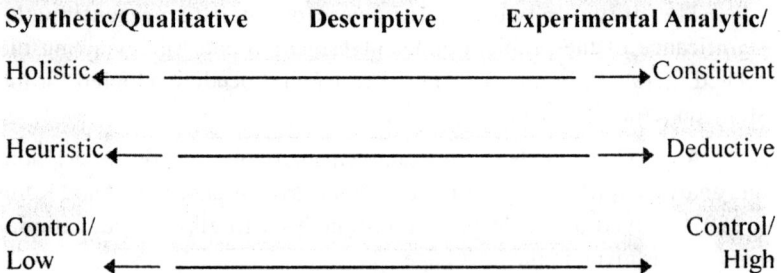

Synthetic/Qualitative	Descriptive	Experimental Analytic/
Holistic ←	——————————————	→ Constituent
Heuristic ←	——————————————	→ Deductive
Control/ Low ←	——————————————	→ Control/ High

Fig 3.1 Types of Designs and the Reserach Parameters
(Selinger and Shohasmy, Research Methods, 1989)

Best and Kahn (1996) have observed that an investigation could be strengthened by implementing Qualitative Approach with the Quantitative approach. Thus, combination of Experimental and Descriptive Research methods and Quantitative and Qualitative approaches employed by the investigator has been proved to be appropriate and warranted.

Table 3.1   Characteristics of Quantitative and Qualitative Reserch (Merriam, 1988)

Points of Comparison	Quantitative	Qualitative
Focus on Research	Quantity (how much, how many)	Quality (mature, essence)
Philosophical Roots	Positivism, Logical Empiricism	Phenomenology, Symbolic Interaction
Associated Phrases	Empirical, Statistical and Experimental	Fieldwork, Ethnographic, Naturalistic, Grounded, Subjective
Goal of Investigation	Description, Confirmation, Prediction, Control, Hypothesis-testing	Understanding, Description, Discovery, Hypothesis-generating
Design Characteristics	Structured, Predetermined	Flexible, Evolving, Emergent
Setting	Unfamiliar, Artificial	Natural, Familiar
Sample	Large, Random, Representative	Small, Non-random, Theoretical
Data Collection	Inanimate Instruments (Scales, Tests, Surveys, Questionnaires, Computers)	Researcher as Primary Instrument, Interviews Observations
Mode of Analysis	Deductive (by Statistical Methods)	Inductive (by Researcher)
Findings	Precise, Narrow, Reductionist	Comprehensive, Holistic, Expansive

BASES OF EXPERIMENTAL METHOD

Experiment is rightly described as 'a question put to nature', the answer to which may be a yes, no or an evasion. A good experimental set-up will minimize the scope for evasion.

The law of the single variable formulated by J.S. Mill cited by Lokesh Koul (2000) is the basic assumption behind the experimentation. The law states that if two situations are similar in every respect and one element is added to or subtracted from one situation but not the other, any difference that develops is the result of the operation of that element added or subtracted.

J.S Mill further gives five modes of discovering and verifying laws of nature as canons or rules. They are

❖   Method of Agreement

❖   Method of Difference.

❖   Joint Method of Agreement and Difference.

❖   Method of Residues.

❖   Method of Concomitant Variations.

The contribution of R.A. Fisher cited in Mangal (2002) in terms of his concept of achieving pre-experimental equation of conditions through random selection of subjects and random assignment of treatments have provided an effective and sound method of conducting realistic experiments with human beings. His techniques of analyses of variance and co-variance made it possible to study complex interactions through factorial designs.

There are four essential characteristics of experimental research:

(i) Control (ii) Manipulation (iii) Observation and (iv) Replication

PROCEDURE OF EXPERIMENT

Every experiment whether it is closed or open involves a series of inter linked steps leading to the completion of the experimental tasks. These steps start with the selection of sample upon which the experiment is conducted and ends with the interpretation of experiment, which is aimed to determine the effectiveness of Reciprocal Teaching. The procedural steps are illustrated in the flow chart given in Fig 3.2

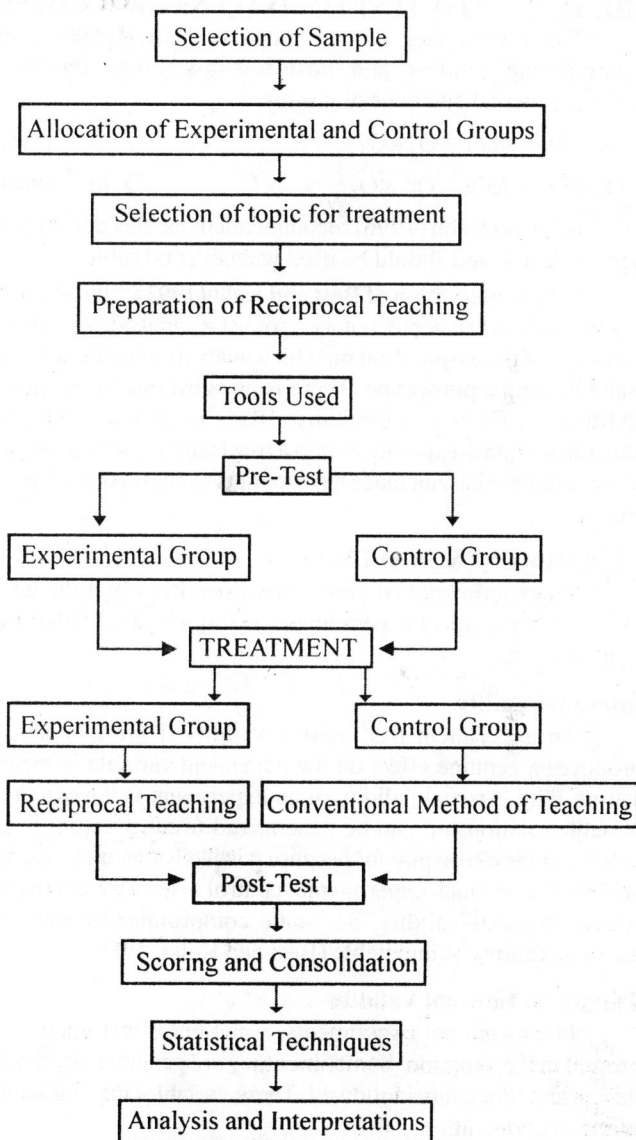

Fig 3.2 Flow Chart showing the Procedure of the Experiment

PRE-TEST - POST-TEST EQUIVALENT GROUP DESIGN

The investigator used a popular classical experimental design, incorporating pre-test and post test assigning subjects randomly to the experimental and control groups.

$R \; O_1 \times O_2 \times gain = O_2 - O_1$ $O_1 \, O_3$ = pretest

$R \; O_3 \times O_4 \times gain = O_4 - O_3$ $O_2 \, O_4$ = posttest

Best and Kahn (1996) recommended that this design is the strongest type of design and should be used whenever possible

In the observation of Best and Kahn(1993), "It should be noted that analysis of covariance is not as a robust as analysis of variance. That is, violation of the assumption on which analysis of covariance is based may make its use inappropriate. There is no substitute for randomization". In addition, as Glass and Hopkins (1984) point out, ANCOVA does not transform a quasi-experiment into a true (randomized) experiment. Hence, the investigator has not made any attempts to apply ANCOVA as a statistical analysis.

EXPERIMENTAL VALIDITY

An experiment can yield honest results only if the design is valid. There are two types of experimental validity - Internal Validity and External Validity.

Internal Validity

An experiment has internal validity if the independent variable produces a genuine effect on the dependent variable in the experimental setting. The external validity of an experiment is the extent to which the variable relationship can be generalized to other settings. Experimental validity is ideal to aspire for because it is likely that it cannot be completely achieved. Too much experimental control to achieve internal validity may reduce external validity. So, some compromise between internal and external validity is inevitable (Best and Kahn, 1989).

Threats to Internal Validity

In educational experiments, a number of extraneous variables are present in the situation. Sometimes they are generated by the experimental design and procedures followed. These variables may influence the results of the experiment.

Before claiming that the selected independent variable has affected the dependent variable, it must be ascertained that the following variables do not produce the effect, which can be mistaken to be the effect of independent variable.

In the present investigation, it was attempted to minimize the threat to internal validity caused by the variables in the manner described below:

(i) History, Maturation and Mortality.

The short duration of the Reciprocal Teaching schedule (30 minutes) and period of the total experiment (twenty days) helped to ensure that the change in subjects was due to Reciprocal Teaching and not due to maturation. No specific incident was noticed during the experimental period that could have influenced the students. Mortality was not a problem in an earlier study of Halpern and Ligget (1984) on '*Computers and Composing: How the new technologies are changing writing*'. In another study by O'Hare (1993) on '*Sentence-combining: Improving student writing without formal grammar instruction*', only one student left the study because the particular student withdrew from the school. In the case of the present study, no student dropped out of the schedule. Hence the effect due to above-mentioned three influences was minimized to a large extent.

(ii) Instrumentation

The willingness scale and reaction scale used were standardized by the investigator and reliability was found to be in the accepted range.

(iii) Selection Bias

Random selection of schools and random assignment of treatments maintained the equivalence between groups to the extent possible.

Threats to External Validity

If the experimental situation is over controlled, it becomes artificial and results become meaningless and inapplicable. The main threat to external validity arises from over control.

Since the experiment was conducted in the actual classroom conditions, threat to external validity arising from artificial laboratory conditions was at the minimum level.

(i) Interaction of Selection and Treatment

This was minimized because no scope was given for voluntary assignment of subjects and samples were drawn from elementary school students.

(ii) Hawthorne Effect and Artificiality of Experimental Setting

The Hawthorne effect is a particular problem when an attempt is made to assess the effect of a new educational technique by comparing it with the old one. The students who get the new technique will apply themselves with more enthusiasm and will therefore learn better from it, just because they are in an experiment. The way to avoid the Hawthorne effect is to arrange things so that the students do not know they are in an experiment. The present study minimized the Hawthorne effect due to these variables by conducting the treatments in the actual classroom, during regular class hours, and by utilizing the services of the respective teachers. This ensured normalcy of treatment procedures.

The investigator applied the 'refined random sample grouping' suggested by Roger Mitton (Practical Research, International Extension College, 1982). The random assignment of students to either of the Reciprocal Teaching Group (Experimental Group) and the Conventional Method Group (Control Group) was refined by 'matching'. The base for matching was the students' performance in their previous year Annual Examinations. The annual examination results were taken as a premise, as it is possible to compare the performance of students through examination results, as evidenced by Karpaga Kumaravel (1993). In the Indian context, the importance given to the examination results and pass percentages is well evident. Many research studies have already been conducted in India and abroad taking the school examination results as the yardstick for achievement (Klitgaard and Hall, 1974; Good and Brophy, 1988 and Kamalamani and Mani, 2002). As the VII standard examination question papers are centrally developed and validated for all the schools in a particular education district, they may reasonably be assumed to be valid. The scores of the students on the basis of which they have been matched to form the sample for the present study may also be assumed to be reliable, as the answer scripts are valued by teachers objectively directly under the supervision of the Head Masters and Assistant Educational Officers.

The students were grouped into pairs of approximately equal ability. Then, each pair was taken in turn and a coin was tossed to decide which student should go into Experimental Group and which student into the Control Group. This matching procedure led to the formation of two intact groups for Treatment A (Control Group -Conventional Method of Teaching) and Treatment B (Experimental Group - Reciprocal Teaching.)

Since the experiment was conducted using pre-test-post-test equivalent groups experimental design, it is very important to examine whether the experimental and control groups are equivalent in all possible aspects or not. In this experimental context, the equivalence of the two groups has been established statistically. Test of significance of difference between means of the Experimental Group and the Control Group with regard to the scores on the pre-test is used for this purpose. Results were interpreted using the two-tailed test of significance for appropriate degrees of freedom. The means, standard deviations and the critical ratios for the scores on Pre-Test between the Experimental group and the Control group were calculated. The data and results of the test of significance of difference between means are summarized and presented in Table 3.2.

Table 3.2 Significance of Difference Pre-Test Scores between Experimental Group and Control Group

Variable	Groups Compared	Total				
		N	M	SD	V	t
Pre-Test	Experimental	400	39.20	22.63	55.18	0.55*
	Control	400	38.60	20.25	52.46	

*Not significant at 0.05 level

The results indicate that there is no significant difference between the Control Group and the Experimental Group in terms of their entry behaviour as measured by the Pre-Test.

SELECTION OF VARIABLES

Variables are the conditions or characteristics that the experimenter manipulates, controls or observes. The independent variables are the conditions or characteristics that the experimenter manipulates or controls in his or her attempt to ascertain their relationship to observed phenomena. The dependent variables are the conditions or characteristics that appear, disappear, or change as the experimenter introduces, removes, or changes independent variables. Reciprocal Teaching Technique and Conventional Method of Teaching were the independent variables. Reading Comprehension Score, Reading Speed Score and Vocabulary Test Score were considered as the dependent variables.

Basal Variables

These independent variables cannot be manipulated by the investigator in the sense that they are less alterable by the investigator. There is another category of independent variables, can be manipulated by the investigator otherwise called as the treatment variables or experimental variables. The investigator can take decisions whether to include independent variables, which cannot be manipulated. This group of variables is methodologically called by the name organismic or attribute variables. Sex of the Sample, Type of Management, Locality, Socio-Economic Status, Exposure to Newspaper and Magazines and Language Interest were the basal variables for the study. Basal variables are independent variables with a difference.

Randomization, Matching the two groups and Statistical balancing were the procedures adopted for controlling the confounding variables.

RESEARCH QUESTIONS

The main objective of the present experimental study was to find out the effectiveness of Reciprocal Teaching of reading over the conventional method of teaching reading in Tamil to the students of 8th Standard. The experiment was designed and carried out to find out answers to the following questions:

1. Is there any advantage in favour of the experimental or control group with regard to the comparison of reading improvement in Tamil at the elementary level?

2. Is there any significant difference in the reading comprehension level as a result of Reciprocal Teaching, of the sub-samples based on Sex, Locality, Type of Management, Socio-Economic Status, Exposure to Newspapers and Magazines and Language Interest? The present study sought to find answerers to the above research questions related to and derived from the objectives of the study.

OBJECTIVES OF THE STUDY

The present experiment was intended to study the effectiveness of Reciprocal Teaching of improving Reading in Tamil at the elementary level over the Conventional Method of Teaching Reading. The changes in Achievement, if any, have been explained in comparison with the Conventional Method of Teaching Reading in Tamil. The specific objectives, which have been formulated for the present study, are presented below with a view to get clear understanding about the purpose of this experiment.

Finding answers to the above questions required the formulation of specific objectives for the experiment in a more precise, research-oriented style as given below:

1. To compare the mean reading comprehension scores of Experimental group and Control group.

2. To compare the mean gain scores of the Experimental group and those of the Control group for the total sample and sub samples.

3. To qualitatively analyse the effect of Reciprocal Teaching Technique on teachers and students.

4. To offer suggestions and recommendations on the basis of the findings of the experiment.

HYPOTHESES

In an experimental study, it is necessary for the experimenters to have certain assumptions regarding the outcome expected of the experiment. These assumptions are framed by the experimenters in tune with the purposes of the investigation. They are technically called by the experts as hypotheses. A hypothesis is something, which is formulated before the final word (hypo = before/below; thesis = final/last word). It is considered as the lifeblood of the investigation. The investigator formulated the hypotheses on the basis of the experiences and familiarity with the topic under examination.

The specific hypotheses formulated on the basis of the insights gained from the review of related literature and tested by the experiment are given below:

1. There will be significant difference between the mean achievement scores of the experimental and those of control group students.

2. There will be significant difference in the mean gain scores between the experimental and those of control group students.

3. The pupils taught through Reciprocal Teaching Technique will have high mean achievement than the pupils taught through conventional methods of teaching.

SAMPLE FOR THE STUDY

Prior to attempting a statement of the sampling technique, an analysis of the distribution of Schools by Management in Tamil Nadu will be relevant. The Tamil Nadu Government's Policy Note on Education for 1999-2000 shows that about 80 per cent of elementary schools are under the state. But primary and middle schools are unequally distributed across the districts, with the maximum number of primary schools in low-literacy districts in Tamil Nadu.

During the five years from 1985 to 1990, despite a policy decision conveyed by the state's slogan 'no more elementary school, no more college', probably to avoid mushrooming of educational institutions and to improve existing institutions, elementary schools were established in localities with predominantly backward population.

Population for the study covers the pupils of Elementary schools in Lalgudi Educational District, falling within the boundaries of Tiruchirappalli Revenue District in the state of Tamil Nadu. For experimentation, pupils of VIII standard were selected. Care was taken to ensure that the subjects selected are equivalent in many respects. The following points were considered for selection of subjects for the experiment.

Rural-Urban Locality: Rural and urban subjects were selected in 1:1 proportion.

Boys-Girls: Equal number of boys and girls from co-educational elementary schools were selected to form the sample.

Type of Management: In the selection of schools, the type of management was also a point of consideration and students from government, government aided and panchayat union schools were selected as subjects for the study.

Based on the above criteria, it was decided to select ten co-educational VIII standard classes from the middle schools and high schools of Lalgudi Educational District of Tamil Nadu state, using Proportionate Stratified Random Sampling.

Two VIII standard classes from each of the ten schools were selected at random. Though some classes were large-sized, 40 students (20 boys and 20 girls) from each class, amounting to 400 boys and 400 girls formed the sample. 200 boys and 200 girls formed the Experimental Group and the rest i.e., 200 boys and 200 girls formed the Control Group. Thus two instact groups of Four Hundred VIII standard students formed the Experimental Group, named Reciprocal Teaching Group (RTG) and the Control Group named Conventional Method Group(CMG), as shown in the following table.

Table 3.3 Distribution of the Sample between the Experimental Group and the Control Group in terms of Sex

Nature of Group	Sex	No. of Students
Reciprocal Teaching Group	Boys	200
(Experimental Group)	Girls	200
Conventional Method Group	Boys	200
(Control Group)	Girls	200

The break-up of the schools in terms of the type of management is given in the Table 3.4.

Table 3.4 Distribution of the Sample between the Experimental Group and the Control Group in terms of type of managementX schools.

Type of School	No. of Schools	No. of Students
Panchayat Union	7	560
State Government	2	160
Private Aided	1	80

RECIPROCAL TEACHING TREATMENT

Reciprocal teaching is an instructional procedure designed to enhance students' comprehension of text. The procedure was designed by Anne Marie Palincsar from Michigan State University and Anne Brown from the University of Illinois. It is characterized by:

- ❖ a dialogue between students and teacher, each taking a turn in the role of dialogue leader;

- ❖ "reciprocal": interactions where one person acts in response to the other;

- ❖ structured dialogue using four strategies: predicting, questioning, summarizing and clarifying.

Each of these strategies helps students to construct meaning from text and monitor their reading to ensure that they in fact understand what they read.

Strategies of Reciprocal Teaching

Predicting: This strategy requires the reader to hypothesize about what the author might discuss next in the text. This provides a purpose for reading: to confirm or disapprove their hypotheses. An opportunity has been created for the students to link the new knowledge they will encounter in the text with the knowledge they already possess. It also facilitates the use of text structure as students learn that headings, subheadings, and questions imbedded in the text are useful means of anticipating what might occur next.

Summarizing: This strategy provides the opportunity to identify, paraphrase and integrate important information in the text.

Questioning: When students generate questions, they first identify the kind of information that is significant enough that it could provide the substance for a question. Then they pose this information in a question form and self—test to ascertain that they can indeed answer their own question.

Clarifying: When teaching students to clarify, their attention is called to the many reasons why text is difficult to understand - for example new vocabulary, unclear referent words and unfamiliar or difficult concepts. Recognizing these blocks to understanding signals the reader to reread, read ahead, or ask for help.

Method of Using the Strategies in a Reading Session

The discussion leader generates predictions in preparation for moving on to the text. The leader then summarizes the text and asks other members if they would like to elaborate upon or revise the summary. Then he/she generates questions to which the group responds. Additional questions are raised by other members of the group. As the last stage, clarifications are discussed.

Introduction of the Strategies to the Students

◈   During the initial phase of instruction the teacher assumes primary responsibility for leading the dialogues and implementing the strategies.

◈   Through modelling, the teacher demonstrates how to use the strategies while reading text.

◈   During guided practice, the teacher supports students by adjusting the demands of the task based on each student's level of proficiency.

◈   Eventually the students learn to conduct the dialogues with little or no teacher assistance.

◈   The teacher assumes the role of a coach/facilitator by providing students with evaluative information regarding their performance and prompting them to higher levels of participation.

Grouping Students for Reciprocal Teaching

Students are taught in small heterogeneous groups to ensure that each student has ample opportunity to practise using the strategies while receiving feedback from other group members. The optimal group size is between six to eight students. Frequent guided practice is essential in helping students become more proficient in their use of the strategies.

Reciprocal Teaching as a Treatment in the Present Study

The following steps were carefully chosen for the students to undergo so that they could use reading comprehension strategies independently, including text prediction, summarization, question generation and clarification of unknown or unclear content.

- ❖ Overhead transparencies of practice reading passages and student copies of the same were prepared. The reading passages in expository style were chosen, keeping in mind, various factors like, human interest and vocabulary suitable for the elementary students and the difficulty level of the text. Reciprocal Teaching Strategies Worksheets were prepared so as to take the students through the four strategies/stages of Reciprocal Teaching.

- ❖ Four successive instructional days were used to introduce each of the following comprehension strategies:

  Day 1 : Prediction

  Day 2 : Summarisation

  Day 3 : Question Generation

  Day 4 : Clarifying

As each strategy was introduced, the responses of students, related to their understanding of key concepts were recorded.

- ❖ After the introduction phase, a review for each strategy was conducted. Then, a student 'instructor' was randomly selected to guide the group to apply the strategy.

- ❖ As the group showed an increased mastery of the strategies, students were assigned to read text segments silently, going through all the four strategies and making relevant entries in the Reciprocal Teaching Strategies Worksheet, a specimen copy of which is given below.

❖   In the choice of reading passage, the group was allowed to vote for a preferred passage from among several possible choices.

❖   The students who became proficient in using the Reciprocal Teaching Technique were assigned as peer tutors to train other students to use Reciprocal Teaching Strategies.

❖   Discussions were promoted among the students to exchange their experiences regarding the application of strategies.

RECIPROCAL TEACHING STRATEGIES WORKSHEET

Student Name: _____

Topic of the Reading Passage _____

1. Predicting. Before you begin to read the selection, look at the main title, the major headings, sub-headings and illustrations. Write down your prediction about what the passage will cover.

_____

_____

_____

2. Summarising. As you finish reading each paragraph or key section of the passage, summarize the main idea of that paragraph or section in one or two complete sentences. (Use the back of this sheet if needed)	**3. Questioning.** For each main idea listed, write down at least one question that the main idea will answer. Good questions should include words like "who", "where", "when", "why", and "what"
❖ **Main idea 1:**_____ _____ _____	❖ **Question 1:**_____ _____ _____
❖ **Main idea 2:**_____ _____ _____	❖ **Question 2:**_____ _____ _____
❖ **Main idea 3:**_____ _____ _____	❖ **Question 3:**_____ _____ _____

IV. Clarifying. Copy down any words, phrases, or sentences in the passage that are unclear:

_____

_____

_____

_____

_____

_____

Cautionary Steps Taken

The possibility of misinformation being given during student discussions was controlled by careful monitoring and timely intervention by the teachers. In situations of Group Instruction and Interactive Learning like that of Reciprocal Teaching context, there is a possibility that the students fail to use the strategies in their independent reading. In order to control this, the teachers walked around the room, observing discussions, checking the students' progress as recorded in their Reciprocal Teaching Strategies Worksheet, discovering the problems faced by the students and offering solutions to their problems with tips for managing such problems independently.

EXPERIMENTATION

A headmasters' meeting was organized at Lalgudi to orient the headmasters of the schools, selected as sample for the present study towards Reciprocal Teaching Technique. The above meeting drew a lot of enthusiasm, as evidenced by the participation of the Joint Director, the Chief Educational Officer and the District Educational Officer. At the second stage, a two-day research workshop on Reciprocal Teaching Technique was organized at Lalgudi to train the teachers who were to practise Reciprocal Teaching Technique for the present study. The schedule of the workshop is as follwrs:

The Experimental Group (RTG) and the Control Group (CMG) were administered the pre-test before introducing the treatment. The Experimental Group (RTG) was taught reading through Reciprocal Teaching Technique. The Conventional Method Group (CMG) was taught reading through conventional method of teaching. The groups were taught

RECIPROCAL TEACHING TECHNIQUE WORKSHOP - SCHEDULE

Reciprocal Teaching Training Day 1 Full Day Training of RT	Reciprocal Teaching Training Day 2 Implementing RT
Session 1	**Session 1**
Introduction	Ice Breaker & Question and Answer from Day 1
	Whole Group Activity
Testimonial: RT Teachers	Topic: Teamwork and Management Strategies
Session 2	**Session 2**
Programme Training: RT Trainer	Whole Group Activity Topics:
Programme Facilitators: RT Core Teachers	◈ Grouping Strategies Example
	◈ Lesson Using RT Skills/ Grouping
	◈ Strategies Discussions
	Demonstration Session
	Differentiation Strategies in RT
Session 3	**Session 3**
Break Out Sessions: General and Content Areas.	Break-out Sessions
	Part 1- Whole Group Grade Level Activity
Materials to be Utilized - Use of Reciprocal Teaching Strategies Worksheet for the steps to be followed by the students while reading	Part 2 - Content level Group Activity
	◈ Share/Review/Discuss ideas for RT implementation using curriculum materials.
	◈ Develop pacing guide for quarter one
	Wrap-Up Question and Answer Activity

reading for twenty days for the duration of thirty minutes each. Post-test was administered to both the groups immediately after the treatment.

CONVENTIONAL LECTURE METHOD

The Conventional Lecture Method continues to be one of the chief methods of teaching even after the availability of the sophisticated media like TV, computers etc. The reasons behind the success of this method are use of apt language, mannerism, wit and humour, skill of drawing attention of the audience, explanation and exposure of the concepts in coherent manner etc. It is a flexible method as teachers can adapt themselves to the subject matter, achievement level of the students, time limit, available apparatus and equipment and all these in a very short notice. While lecturing, the teacher can get reinforcement from the students in terms of their attention. Students' attention and interest can be captured by teacher's wit and humour, non-verbal communications such as gestures, posture and movement, logical statements and enthusiasm. In addition, the physical environment of the lecture hall itself may give security to some students as they are doing the right thing by being present along with their classmates at the right place, at right time and respond to the teacher in one way or other. In addition to the students' gaining knowledge and comprehending the subject matter, lectures also provide group feelings, social reinforcement and emotional security. All these considerations are the advantages of lecture method and thereby account for importance and continuance.

For the present study, Lesson Plans for teaching through the Conventional Method to the Control Group were prepared on the basis of International objectives of Teaching Reading in Tamil, the curriculum Guidelines of the Department of Education, Government of Tamil Nadu and recommendations of National Council for Educational Research and Training. The objectives were fixed in observable and measurable behavioural terms. The content was analyzed into facts and concepts. On the basis of the analysis of content, the entry behaviour of the pupils were identified.

INSTRUMENTATION

Tools with proven psychomatric properties to measure the intended variables have been developed and used by the investigator. A brief description of these tools is presented in this part.

PSK READING SKILL TEST

The PSK Silent Reading Test was constructed to measure the attainment of pupils in the elementary classes in the skill of silent reading of the work-study type.

The test is grouped into three parts, each measuring a particular area of silent reading abilities namely (1) Comprehension of words, sentences and paragraphs; (2) Reading Speed at a controlled level of comprehension; and (3) Acquisition of vocabulary.

Selection of the Skills to be Measured, Development, and Standardization of the test:

Efficient reading implies clear comprehension of the communication presented in print or writing in a reasonably speeded form Comprehension and rate of reading are the two main factors leading to efficiency in reading. Reading efficiency involves a whole repertoire of skills.

The unit skills measured by the PSK Reading Skills Test are as follows:

Test 1   -   Reading Comprehension

Test 2   -   Reading Speed

Test 3   -   Vocabulary.

Test 1: Reading Comprehension

The ultimate aim of all reading is comprehension. Bhagya Lakshmi and Rao (2000) quote the definition of comprehension by Macmillan(1965), "understanding what is written within, between and beyond the lines". Reading comprehension carries the understanding of a word or a phrase by reading and recognition of the meaning intended by the author. It also involves determining the meaning of words in the sentence and meaning of the sentence in relation to the passage. More often than not, this end product is measured by carefully chosen questions to test the pupils' ability to identify and understand details essential to the meaning of the passage.

Test 2: Reading Speed

Ahuja and Ahuja (1991) quote Hafner and Jolly (1956) "An efficient reading rate is the maximum unforced speed that a reader can employ to get the desired meaning from the context". The meaningful measurement of reading speed involves the control of the comprehension level at which the reading takes place. In this part of the test, pupils are asked to read a passage at a rate, which, for them is best for clear comprehension. They were asked to make note of the starting time and the closing time. The time taken for reading the passage is calculated. The reading speed was calculated in terms of words per minute (w.p.m), using the following formula, developed byVenkata Iyer (1986) and applied by many researchers including Bhagya Lakshmi and Rao (2000).

$$\left[\frac{\text{No. of words}}{\text{Total time take in seconds}} \right] \times 60 = \text{Speed in words per minute}$$

In this part of the test, the students were given a new, untaught passage, chosen from the VIII standard Social Science textbook to read and comprehend. The passage was followed by sixteen questions related to the main ideas, supporting details and concepts underlying the information.

Test 3: Vocabulary:

The most significant of all factors, impeding reading speed and comprehension is poor vocabulary. Rich vocabulary is a means and end of efficient reading. Many standardized tests, including the Edinburgh Reading Tests (1977) developed at the University of Edinburgh have test of vocabulary as sub test and much of the focus is on technical/semi technical vocabulary found in the text.

In this part of the test, used for the present study, the students were subjected to a test of vocabulary. A new, untaught passage, containing vocabulary of semi technical category, from the VIII standard Social Science text book was given and the six questions that followed aimed at testing the students' understanding and appropriate use of the semi technical vocabulary found in the text.

VARIOUS STAGES IN THE CONSTRUCTION OF TOOL

Planning the Test:

Before making an attempt to construct tools to test the skills of reading, it was considered desirable to locate and analyse the available tools. The search in the literature revealed that no tool is available in India that could measure reading skills in Tamil with specific reference to the elementary stage. Hence a tool was developed for the purpose and the construction of tool underwent the following developmental stages:

Preparing the Test Items:

For the identification of conceptual aspects, the investigator made an extensive review of the related books.

In the process of constructing the tools, the investigator also drew heavily upon the following available standard foreign tools for conceptual aspects:

◈   IOWA Silent Reading Test, 1942

◈   SRA Reading Test, 1959

◈   Durrel-Sullivan Reading Capacity and Achievement Test, 1965

◈   Stanford Diagnostic Reading Test, 1966

◈   The Edinburgh Reading Test, 1977

Expert opinions from 10 Tamil Teachers and 10 Reading Evaluation Experts and Pronouncement of the National Council of Educational Research and Training and District Primary Education Project (DPEP) on the Minimum Levels of Learning and Competency based learning at the elementary stage were also taken into consideration in finalizing the items on different dimensions of the reading skills.

Reviewing the Items

The developed tool was presented to a panel of 10 judges including Professors of Tanjore Tamil University, Central Institute of Indian Languages, the Department of Tamil studies, Bharathidasan University and the Department of Educational Technology, Bharathidasan University in order to check whether the test is based upon a careful analysis of the skills to be tested and whether the items represented adequately each portion of the analysis not just those aspects which lend themselves most readily to a particular kind of test question. On the basis of the recommendations made by the judges, defects in certain items were corrected.

The modified test was presented to a group of 10 Elementary Class teachers for their critique and additional input.

Pilot Study and Item Analysis

The completed test was subjected to a pilot study on a sample of 100 students. Sufficient time for all the testees to attempt every item was allowed in the Pilot Study. The immediate purpose of an item analysis is to determine the difficulty and discrimination indices of each item, to be included in the final study. The D-Index method suggested by Stanely et.al. (1978) and Valette (1977) was followed in doing the item analysis, because of its simplicity.

Determining Item Difficulty

Based on the scores obtained by the pupils in the Pilot Study tests, the high and the low groups were defined using 27 percent cutting point. The top 27 per cent of the pupils formed the high group and the bottom 27 per cent of the pupils formed the low group.

As the item-analysis proceeds, four figures were recorded for each item:

H - number of highs who answered correctly.

L - number of lows who answered correctly.

H+L - total number who answered correctly (success)

H-L - how many more highs than lows answered correctly (discrimination)

Item-wise analysis was made to find out the proportion of the pupils who answered each item correctly in the high and the low groups. These were denoted by PH and PL. Using these values, the item difficulty level P was obtained by the formula:

$$P = \frac{PH + PL}{2}$$

Determining Item Discrimination

The item discrimination D was obtained by using the formula: D = (PH - PL)

Ebel (1979) is of the opinion that an item with the index of discrimination 0.35 and up can be considered a very good item. Lindeman and Merenda (1979) observed: "Since the test maker should usually strive to achieve high discriminating power, most items should have difficulty levels between 0.40 and 0.60". Taking into account these facts, items having highest discrimination indices and difficulty levels between 0.40 and 0.60 were selected. The survived items were arranged according to their difficulty and discrimination indices.

Determining the Effectiveness of Distracters

In the test items, which are of multiple-choice type, one further step was made in the item analysis namely inspecting the way each item's distracters functioned. If an item contains a distracter, which attracted no one, not even the poorest testees, it is a non-functioning distracter. If a "wrong" distracter attracted more high than low scores, it is a malfunctioning distracter. Retaining such a distracter will actually harm the test. As non-functioning and malfunctioning distracters were not found in the analysis of all the items, there was no need to make any alterations in the distracters.

The usable items thus selected were assembled in the final form.

Establishment of Reliability

"The reliability of a test refers to the consistency of scores obtained by the same individuals on different occasions or with different sets of equivalent items". (Anastasi, 1954). One of the first requirements of the test is internal consistency or reliability.

There are four methods to estimate and determine the reliability of the test. They are (1) Test Retest Method, (2) Alternate or Parallel Forms Method, (3) Split- Half Technique and (4) Rational Equivalence.

The limitation of the test-retest method is that if the time interval between the two tests is relatively short, the testees' memories of their previous responses will make their two performances spuriously consistent and thus lead to an overestimate of test reliability. On the other hand, if the time interval is so long as to minimize the "memory factor", the testees' reading skills under study may have undergone a genuine change, producing different responses to the same items, and thus the test reliability could be underestimated.

The second method of computing reliability with the use of alternate or parallel form was not attempted by the investigator because equivalent forms of these tests are not available as already mentioned. "The Split-half method is regarded by many as the best of the methods for measuring test reliability. One of its main advantages is the fact that all data for computing reliability are obtained upon one occasion so that variations brought about by differences between the two testing situations are eliminated" (Garrett, 1959). As suggested by Garret, the split-half method of computing reliability was attempted in the present study.

Each test was divided into two halves by separating the odd and even numbered items, obtaining two scores for each individual. The correlation between the results of the two halves was compounded. As this correlation value is not directly applicable to the full length test which is the actual instrument prepared for use, Spearman Brown Prophecy Formula was used to estimate the reliability of the full length test from the self correlation of the half-tests. The Spearman Brown Prophecy Formula used and its description are given below:

$$r_{11} = \frac{2r}{1+r}$$

r_{11} = reliability co-efficient for the full length test.

r = reliability co-efficient of the half test found experimentally.

Table 3.5 Reliability Co-Efficients for the PSK Reading Tkill Test in Tamil

Section	Description of the Sub-skills	Split half Co-efficients	Corrected to full length by Spearman Brown Formula
A	Reading Speed	0.81	0.89
B	Reading Comprehension	0.93	0.97
C	Vocabulary	0.82	0.90

Establishment of Validity

"The validity of a test depends upon the fidelity with which it measures what it purports to measure" (Garrett, 1971).

The face validity of the present tool was established by the fact that the test was constructed by methods suggested and endorsed by eminent people and experienced teachers in the field.

The content validity was also established since an analysis was first made of the skill itself and decisions were made on what dimensions of the skills need to be tested, and in what proportions. As the analysis and the resultant tests accord with the views of recognized authorities in the areas of reading and language testing, the tests can be said to have content validity.

The empirical validation of the test scores against external criterion cold not be done, and there were no comparable standard tools on reading skills in India particulary for the elementary stage in the state of Tamil Nadu.

Scoring

Correction for chance success, for such of those items having multiple responses, was made using the formula given by Lindman (1971)

$$Sc = R - \frac{W}{n-1}$$

Where Sc = Corrected Score

R = Right response

W = Wrong response

n = number of alternatives

Prior to the introduction of the treatment, the PSK Reading Skill Test was administered as a Pre-Test in all the 10 schools selected. This data ensured the entry status of the students in terms of the Reading Skill Score with regard to his/her Reading Comprehension, Reading Speed and Acquisition of Vocabulary. The Post Test data were collected from the subject both in the Experimental and Control Group after the completion of the treatments. This was with a view to quantifying the terminal characteristics of the subjects in terms of Reading Skill Score in Tamil. For this purpose, the PSK Reading Skill Test constructed by the investigator already used in the Pre-Test was made use of. Before administration, all necessary guidelines were given to the subjects both in the Experimental and Control Group about the Post-Test and the purpose of which was made clear to them. An analysis of the responses for this PSK Reading Skill Test is made in Chapter IV.

SOCIO-ECONOMIC STATUS SCALE

A Socio-Economic Status Scale was used for collecting information about the Socio-Economic Status of the subjects. This standardized tool is the modified form of the widely used Socio-Economic Status Scale of Kuppuswamy, adopted by Karpaga Kumaravel (1993). This scale consists of three parts (a) Education, (b) Occupation and (c) Income of the parents. Each of these categories has 7 sub-categories. Total score of the sub-categories checked in each criterion shows the socio-economic status of the subject. The test was validated by using various methods: (a) matching against outside criterion (b) distribution patterns, (c) comparison of dichotomous groups. The time required to complete the scale is a maximum of 10 minutes. Income level of Parents, Parental Education, Parental Occupation - these categories are included in the General Data Sheet. The sub-divisions and weightage of each categories are as follows.

Income Level of Parents	Weightage
Below Rs. 3000	5
Between 3001 - 4000	10
Between 4001 - 5000	15
Between 5001 - 6000	20
Between 6001 - 7000	25
Above Rs.7000	30

Parental Education	Weightage
Not received formal Schooling	5
Standard I - IV	10
Standard V - VII	15
Standard VIII - X	20
PDC, TTC	25
B.C.,/B.Sc.,/B.Com	30
M.B.B.S.,/M.Ed., B.E.,/M.B.A.,/Ph.D./C.A. etc.	

Parental Occupation	Weightage
Unemployed	5
Unskilled	10
Semi Skilled	15
Skilled	20
Semi Professional	25
Professional	30
Highly Professional	35

LANGUAGE INTEREST INVENTORY

Interests are the integral part of one's personality. Interests of an individual yield important information about the makeup of his / her personality. Interest is one of the determinants of the individual differences.

An interest is very much the same as attitude, though their definition is also a matter of controversy. Their subject matter is usually more concrete. One is interested in or like language, athletics, music, model of aeroplanes etc., whereas one has favourable or other attitude towards religion, nationality etc.

Interest inventories attempt to yield a measure of the types of activities that an individual has a tendency to like and to choose. The tools used for describing and measuring interests of individuals are the interest inventories or interest blanks. They are self-report instruments in which the individuals note their own likes and dislikes. They are of the nature of standardized feelings about certain situations and phenomena, which are then interpreted in terms of interests. For the present study, the Language Interest Inventory consisting of 20 different items was used. The subject has to tick mark one of the alternatives i.e., A (for agree), N (for neutral) or D (for dislike) provided against each item.

The development of the Socio Economic Status Scale and the Language Interest Inventory passed through the following main phases: a) Pre-Pilot Phase, (b) Pilot Study and Pre-Test Phase and (c) Finalization Phase. The Pre-Pilot Phase was concerned with the gathering of items related to the constructs under study. The preliminary item pool was generated by drawing from the following sources: 1) an extensive review of literature dealing with various aspects of the concepts taken for the study and 2) formal and informal discussions with experts. The items in the above tools were subjected to screening and debugging. The tools were Pre-Tested with a sample not eventually to be studied. It was found that no major changes were necessary in the content of the tools. Pointing out the difference between the Pilot Study and Pre-Test, Good and Hatt (1983) observed "While the pilot study furnishes an answer to the question 'How does the researcher formulate items in the tool?" the pretest answers the question "How does he finalizes items for the final schedule?" Pre test is a much more formal step than the pilot study. The pre test done by the investigator was a dress rehearsal of the final study. Every part of the inventory was laid out exactly as in the case of the final study, in a nearby institution to know whether they understand the meaning of the items both in terms of content and format and responded accordingly. The investigator has also tabulated the data from the pretest, in order to see what weaknesses are. Suitable changes were made in the format of the questionnaire. The responses of the students to this Language Interest Inventory led to the categorization of the students into three groups, viz., High Language Interest Group, Medium Language Interest Group and Low Language Interest Group.

WILLINGNESS SCALE FOR TEACHERS

To ascertain the willingness of teachers to implement Reciprocal Teaching, the investigator developed and standardized a willingness scale, modeled after the one developed by Passi and Sansanwal (1985). The original scale was a three-point scale and consisted of twenty-two items. A rough draft of items was prepared and circulated among a panel of judges to assess its suitability.

Content validity refers to the degree to which the test actually measures or is specifically related to the traits for which it was designed. A panel of judges comprising of language teachers, teacher educators and experts was chosen. The panel judged the tool's adequacy and some changes were suggested and they were incorporated.

The reliability was determined by using the technique of Split-Half method. The test was divided into two equivalent 'halves' and the correlation was found for the half tests. The odd-even split method was used to split the test. From the reliability of the half test, the correlation of the whole test was determined using the Spearman-Brown Prophecy Formula. The correlation co-efficient of the split half test was 0.61 and the reliability of the whole test was 0.757.

The tool finally used consisted of eighteen items to be rated on a three-point scale - Agree/Neutral/Disagree. The positive statements were scored as three for agree, two for neutral, and one for disagree. The negative items were scored as three for disagree, two for neutral, and one for agree. The maximum score one couldearn was fifty-four.

REACTION SCALE FOR TEACHERS

The feasibility of any educational innovation depends on how the teachers, who participate in it react towards it. Thus the necessity for measuring the reactions of the teachers towards Reciprocal Teaching was felt and a reaction scale was administered after Reciprocal Teaching sessions.

D'Lima and Sugandhi (1986) prepared a reaction scale consisting of twenty-three items to be rated on a five-point scale. The investigator made slight modifications in the original tool to suit the conditions of the present study.

The modified version of the tool was submitted to a panel of judges. The suggestions of the experts were used to incorporate some changes.

The reliability was measured using the odd/even- split-half technique. The correlation co-efficient of the split halves was 0.66 and the reliability co-efficient of the whole test was 0.795.

The final version consisting of sixteen items to be rated on a three-point scale: Agree/Neutral/Disagree was administered. The statements were scored as three for Agree, two for Neutral and one for Disagree for positive statements and vice versa for negative statements. The total score obtainable is forty-eight.

WILLINGNESS SCALE FOR STUDENTS

To ensure the success of trying out any innovation in the process of Teaching and Learning, a deep understanding of the willingness of the students who participate in the innovation is essential. D'Lima and Sugandhi (1986) developed a willingness questionnaire consisting of nine items. The scale was developed to find out the willingness of student teachers who had attended a workshop on Inquiry Training Model.

The investigator developed a scale to find out the willingness of students to adopt Reciprocal Teaching technique in the real life situations. The content validity was established using the expert opinion of a panel of judges. The reliability was measured by split-half technique. The co-efficient of split halves was found to be 0.704 and reliability co-efficient of the whole test was 0.83.

The final scale consisted of fourteen items to be rated on a three-point scale Yes(Willing) / Undecided / No(Unwilling). The statements were scored as three for Agree, two for Neutral and one for Disagree for positive statements and vice versa for negative statements. The total score obtainable is forty-two.

CONCLUSION

Thus the present research design has covered the following phases:

(1) Selection of sample and allocation of Experimental and Control Groups.

(2) Administration of Reciprocal Teaching Treatment.

(3) Administration of relevant Research Tools.

The test scores thus obtained were subjected to analysis and interpretation, which lead to the next chapter.

4
After the Experiment : Analysis and Interpretation of Data

"The challenge before a researcher is to make sense out of massive amount of data, reduce the volume of information, identify significant patterns and construct a framework for communicating the essence of what the data reveal"

(John W Best 1996)

PROLOGUE TO THE ANALYSIS

Analysis of the collected data is a vital component of any research work. Without analysis, which provides a deeper insight into its basic nature, the adequate description of a phenomenon is relatively impossible. Analysis of data means studying the organized material in order to discover inherent facts. The data are studied from as many angles as possible to explore the new facts. Analysis requires an alert, flexible and open-mind. It is worthwhile to prepare a plan of analysis before the actual collection of data. Lokesh Koul (2001) suggests four helpful modes to get started on analyzing the gathered data.

1. To think in terms of significant tables that the data permit.

2. To examine carefully the statement of the problem and earlier analysis and to study the original records of the data.

3. To get away from the data and to think about the problem in layman's terms, or to actually discuss that problem with others.

4. To attack the data by making various statistical calculations.

In this chapter, the procedures undertaken for the processing and analysis of information obtained from the experiment is presented.

Information was processed according to the purpose or objectives of the experiment. This is the major task after the experiment. The whole processing of information was done using computer facilities especially with the Statistical Package for Social Sciences (SPSS). The bulk of information obtained from the experiment was subjected for quantitative as well as qualitative treatments. This involves laborious procedures to be done with care and caution leading to the interpretations of various quantitative and qualitative treatments.

The main purpose of the experiment was to determine the effectiveness of Reciprocal Teaching. Pre-test-Post-test equivalent Group Experimental Design was used to collect the needed data. The data collected and tabulated were processed using three quantitative techniques namely the Test of Significance of Difference between Means, Analysis of Variance and Chi-square. Processing and analysis of information using these quantitative methods are described in this chapter in detail.

ESTABLISHING THE IDENTITY OF CONTROL AND EXPERIMENTAL GROUPS

As the main objective of the study is to compare the relative effectiveness of the Conventional Method and Reciprocal Method of Teaching Reading in Tamil at the elementary level, it is proposed to study and establish the identity of Control and Experimental Groups of the present study. In this empirical verification, the two major groups considered were boys and girls and rural and urban. The reason behind examining the significance of boys-girls and rural-urban achievements is that girls and people hailing from rural areas are discriminated against their counterparts socially and economically. Studies carried out at the Indian Context by Tilak (1984, 1987), Kapoor (1988) and Mehta (1989) empirically proved that the deprived segments of the society namely the rural individuals and girls are discriminated socially, economically and educationally. These discriminations are bound to influence the achievement scores significantly in the study area in terms of the indicators considered for scoring. Hence, the categorization of groups as boys and girls and rural and urban were made.

Null Hypothesis: 1 (H_o1)

There is no significant difference between the means of the Reading

Comprehension scores of Boys and Girls taught through Conventional Method as measured by pre-test.

In order to establish the identity of the Control Group with regard to sex as a variable, the H_O1 was formulated. In order to test this Null Hypothesis, 't' test was attempted between the means of the two Sub-Sample Groups, namely boys and girls as measured by the pre-test.

Table 4.1 Significance of Difference between the Means of the Reading Comprehension Scores of Boys and Girls taught through Conventional Method as measured by Pre-Test

Group	N	Mean	S.D	C.V.	S.E	t
Boys	200	4.5	0.80	17.78	0.76	0.26*
Girls	200	4.7	0.71	15.11		

*Not Significant at 0.5 level

As seen in Table 4.1, the mean scores under Conventional Method in Reading Comprehension for boys and girls stood at 4.5 and 4.7 respectively with a standard deviation of 0.80 and 0.71 respectively. The coefficient of variation, a relative measure of dispersion indicates that the dispersion is more in the case of boys 17.78 per cent than that of girls 15.11 per cent. However, the average score obtained by boys was higher than that of girls. The worked out 't' value indicates that the differences in scores between boys and girls are not significant, as the calculated value of 0.26 is less than the table value of 1.96. Hence, the Null Hypothesis is not rejected and it is concluded that boys and girls do not differ between themselves in terms of the Reading Comprehension scores when they are taught through Conventional Method as measured by pre-test.

Null Hypothesis: 2 (H_O2)

There is no significant difference between the means of the Reading Comprehension scores of rural and urban students taught through Conventional Method as measured by pre-test.

In order to establish the identity of the Control Group with regard to locality as a variable, as measured by Pre-test, the H_O2 was formulated. In order to test this Null Hypothesis, 't' test was attempted between the means of the two Sub-Sample Groups namely rural and urban students as measured by the pre-test.

Table 4.2 Significance of Difference between the Means of the Reading Comprehension Scores of Rural . d Urban Students taught through Conventional Method as measured by Pre-Test

Group	N	Mean	S.D	C.V..	S.E	t
Rural	280	4.35	0.79	18.16	0.75	0.99*
Urban	120	5.10	0.67	13.14		

* Not Significant at 0.5 level

A close perusal of the mean scores provided in Table 4.2 for students of rural and urban areas of the study indicates that while for the rural area the mean score registered was 4.35, it was 5.10 in the case of urban area.

The worked out standard deviation shows that it was 0.79 and 0.67 respectively in the case of rural and urban areas. The coefficient of variation was higher with 18.16 per cent in the rural area and 13.14 per cent in the urban area implying that the dispersion in the scores obtained by the students of rural areas were more when compared to urban area. However, the test statistics indicate that the differences in scoring between rural and urban areas are not significant as the 't' value 0.99 was less than table value. Hence, the Null Hypothesis is not rejected and it is concluded that rural and urban students do not differ between themselves in terms of the Reading Comprehension scores when they are taught through Conventional Method as measured by pre-test.

Null Hypothesis: 3 (H_o3)

There is no significant difference between the means of the Reading Comprehension scores of boys and girls taught through Conventional Method as measured by post-test.

In order to establish the identity of the Control Group with regard to sex as a variable as measured by Post-Test, the H_o3 was formulated. In order to test this Null Hypothesis, 't' test was attempted between the means of the two Sub-Sample Groups namely boys and girls as measured by the post-test.

Tabe 4.3 Significance of Difference between the Means of the Reading Comprehension Scores of Boys and Girls taught through Conventional Method as measured by Post-Test

Group	N	Mean	S.D	C.V..	S.E	t
Boys	200	5.25	0.75	14.29	0.72	1.02*
Girls	200	5.98	0.68	11.37		

*Not Significant at 0.5 level

As provided in Table 4.3, the respective mean scores for the Post-test in Reading Comprehension stood at 5.25 and 5.98 respectively, with a standard deviation of 0.75 and 0.68 respectively. The coefficient of variation registered for these two groups indicate a relatively stable scoring for both boys and girls, though the stability is slightly more for boys 14.29 per cent, when compared to girls 11.37 per cent. The 't' value calculated indicates that the differences in scoring is not significant between boys and girls as the calculated 't' value of 1.02 is slightly lower than the table 't' value of 1.96. Hence the null hypothesis is not rejected and it is concluded that there is no significant difference between the means of the Reading Comprehension scores of boys and girls taught through Conventional Method as measured by Post-test.

Null Hypothesis: 4 ($H_0 4$)

There is no significant difference between the means of the Reading Comprehension scores of rural and urban students taught through Conventional Method as measured by Post-test.

In order to establish the identity of the Control Group with regard to locality as a variable as measured by Post-Test, the $H_0 4$ was formulated. In order to test this Null Hypothesis, 't' test was attempted between the means of the two Sub-Sample Groups namely rural and urban students as measured by the Post-test.

Table 4.4   Significance of Difference between the Means of the Reading Comprehension Scores of Rural and Urban Students taught through Conventional Method as measured by Post-Test

Group	N	Mean	S.D	C.V..	S.E	t
Rural	280	5.33	0.74	13.75		
					0.72	0.83*
Urban	120	5.91	0.66	11.04		

*Not Significant at 0.5 level

A look at the mean values provided in Table 4.4 shows that the mean scores of the urban students of the Conventional Method in the Reading Comprehension as measured by the Post-Test is relatively higher with 5.91 when compared to that of rural students (5.33) implying the better performance of the urban students than their counterparts. The standard deviation and the eventual coefficient of variation worked out also shows a higher instability experienced in scoring by the rural students than the urban students. However, this difference in the mean scores has turned out to be insignificant as the calculated 't' value (0.83) is less than the table 't' value of 1.96. Thus, this test shows that rural and urban students do not differ between themselves in terms of Reading Comprehension Scores when they are taught through conventional method as measured by Post-Test.

Null Hypothesis: 5 (H$_0$5)

There is no significant difference between the means of the Gain Scores of boys and girls of Conventional Method Group in Reading Comprehension.

In order to establish the identity of the Control Group with regard to sex as the variable, the H$_0$5 was formulated. In order to test this Null Hypothesis, 't' test was attempted between the means of the two Sub-Sample Groups namely boys and girls.

Table 4.5 Significance of Difference between the Means of the Gain Scores of Boys and Girls taught through Conventional Method in Reading Comprehension

Group	N	Mean	S.D	C.V..	S.E	t
Boys	200	1.03	0.05	4.85	0.39	0.38*
Girls	200	0.88	0.01	1.14		

*Not Significant at 0.05 level

A close perusal of the mean scores provided in Table 4.5 for boys and girls indicates that the mean gain scores of boys and girls between the pre and Post-Tests were 1.03 and 0.88 respectively. The coefficient of variation registered for these two groups indicate a relatively stable scoring for both boys and girls, though the stability is more for boys 4.85 per cent, when compared to girls 1.14 per cent. The 't' value calculated indicates that the differences in the gains are not significant between boys and girls as the calculated V value of 0.38 is lower than the table 't' value of 1.96. Hence the null hypothesis is not rejected and it is concluded that there is no significant difference between the means of the gain scores of boys and girls in Reading Comprehension between the pre and Post-Tests.

Null Hypothesis: 6(H$_0$6)

There is no significant difference between the means of the Gain Scores of rural and urban students of Conventional Method Group in Reading Comprehension.

In order to establish the identity of the Control Group with regard to locality as a variable, the H$_0$6 was formulated. In order to test this Null

Hypothesis, 't' test was attempted between the means of the two Sub-Sample Groups namely rural and urban students.

Table 4.6 Significance of Difference between the Means of the Gain Scores of Rural and Urban Students taught through Conventional Method in Reading Comprehension

Group	N	Mean	S.D	C.V..	S.E	t
Rural	280	0.75	0.14	18.67	0.1	0.80*
Urban	120	1.28	0.12	9.38		

*Not Significant at 0.5 level

A look at the mean values provided in Table 4.6 shows that the mean gain scores of the urban students of the Conventional Method Group in the Reading Comprehension between the pre and Post-Tests is relatively higher with 1.28 when compared to that of rural students (0.75) implying the better performance of the urban students than their counterparts. The standard deviation and the eventual coefficient of variation worked out also shows a higher instability experienced in scoring by the rural students than the urban students. However, this difference in the mean scores has turned out to be insignificant as the calculated 't' value (0.80) is less than the table 't' value of 1.96. Thus, this test shows that rural and urban students do not differ between themselves in terms of their Gain Scores in Reading Comprehension between the pre and Post-Tests.

Null Hypothesis: 7 (H$_o$7)

There is no significant difference between the means of the Reading Speed scores of boys and girls taught through Conventional Teaching Method as measured by Pre-Test

In order to establish the identity of the Experimental Group with regard to Pre-Test, the H$_O$7 was formulated. In order to test this Null Hypothesis, 't' test was attempted between the means of the two Sub-Sample Groups namely boys and girls.

Table 4.7 Significance of Difference between the Means of the Reading Speed Scores of Boys and Girls taught through Conventional Method as measured by Pre-Test

Group	N	Mean	S.D	C.V..	S.E	t
Boys	200	62.50	12.38	19.81	12.37	0.51*
Girls	200	68.75	12.36	17.98		

*Not Significant at 0.5 level

A close perusal of the data provided in table 4.7 indicates that the mean scores of the boy and girl students stood at 62.50 and 68.75 respectively, with a coefficient of variation of 19.81 per cent and 17.98 per cent respectively. An analysis of the mean scores and the coefficient of variation of the two groups indicate that the girl students have a slight advantage in the mean scores over their male counterparts. This trend is found to be present in the case of coefficient of variation also, that is, the dispersion in the scores of girl students is slightly lower than the male students. This provides the inference that on the average the performance of girl students in the reading speed is better when compared to boys. However, their mean score difference is tested for its significance using the 't' statistics. The calculated value obtained for the means is 0.51. A comparison of the calculated value with that of the table value indicates that the calculated value is less than the table value and hence the null hypothesis that "There is no significant difference between the means of the Reading Speed scores of boys and girls taught through Conventional Teaching Method as measured by Pre-Test" has been accepted.

Null Hypothesis: $8(H_o 8)$

There is no significant difference between the means of the Reading Speed scores of rural and urban students taught through Conventional Teaching Method as measured by Pre-Test.

In order to establish the identity of the Experimental Group with regard to Pre-Test, the $H_o 8$ was formulated. In order to test this Null Hypothesis, 't' test was attempted between the means of the two Sub-Sample Groups namely rural and urban students as measured by Pre-Test.

Table 4.8   Significance of Difference between the Means of the Reading Speed Scores of Rural and Urban Students taught through Conventional Method as measured by Pre-Test

Group	N	Mean	S.D	C.V..	S.E	t
Rural	280	62.74	12.66	20.18	12.38	0.78*
Urban	120	72.38	11.69	16.15		

*Not Significant at 0.05 level

A close look at the mean scores provided in table 4.8 indicates that the mean scores for rural and urban areas stood at 62.74 and 72.38

respectively. The standard deviation for urban and rural students stood respectively at 12.66 and 11.69, indicating more dispersion experienced in the case of rural students than that of the urban students. The coefficient of variation stood at 20.18 per cent and 16.15 per cent respectively for the rural and urban areas. The difference in the mean scores is tested for its significance using the 't' test. For this purpose the null hypothesis has been framed as "there is no significant difference between the means of the Reading Speed scores of rural and urban students taught through Conventional Teaching Method as measured by Pre-Test". The calculated value obtained for the means is 0.78. A comparison of the calculated value with that of the table value indicates that the calculated value is lower than the table value and hence the null hypothesis that "There is no significant difference between the means of the Reading Speed scores of rural and urban students taught through Conventional Teaching Method as measured by Pre test" has been accepted.

Null Hypothesis: 9 (H_O9)

There is no significant difference between the means of the Reading Speed scores of boys and girls taught through Conventional Teaching Method as measured by Post-Test.

In order to establish the identity of the Experimental Group with regard to Post-Test, the H_O9 was formulated. In order to test this Null Hypothesis, 't' test was attempted between the means of the two Sub-Sample Groups namely boys and girls.

Table 4.9 Significance of Difference between the Means of the Reading Speed Scores of Boys and Girls taught through Conventional Method as measured by Post-Test

Group	N	Mean	S.D	C.V.	S.E	t
Boys	200	63.28	11.76	18.58	12.39	0.37*
Girls	200	67.92	12.98	19.11		

*Not Significant at 0.05 level

A close perusal of the data provided in table 4.9 indicates that the mean scores of the boy and girl students stood at 63.28 and 67.92 respectively, with a coefficient of variation of 18.58 per cent and 19.11 per cent respectively. An analysis of the mean scores and the coefficient of variation of the two groups indicate that the girl students have a slight advantage in the mean scores over their male counterparts. This trend is found to be present in the case of coefficient of variation also, that is, the dispersion in the scores of girl students is slightly lower than the male students. This provides the inference that on the average the performance of girl students in the reading speed is better when compared to boys. However, their mean score difference is tested for its significance using the 't' statistics. The calculated value obtained for the means is 0.37. A comparison of the calculated value with that of the table value indicates that the calculated value is less than the table value and hence the null hypothesis that "There is no significant difference between the means of the Reading Speed scores of boys and girls taught through Conventional Teaching Method as measured by Post-Test" has been accepted.

Null Hypothesis: 10 (H_O10)

There is no significant difference between the means of the Reading Speed scores of rural and urban students taught through Conventional Teaching Method as measured by Post test.

In order to establish the identity of the Experimental Group with regard to Post-Test, the H_O10 was formulated. In order to test this Null Hypothesis, 't' test was attempted between the means of the two Sub-Sample Groups namely rural and urban students as measured by Post-Test.

Table 4. 10 Significance of Difference between the Means of the Reading Speed Scores of Rural and Urban Students taught through Conventional Method as measured by Post-Test

Group	N	Mean	S.D	C.V.	S.E	t
Rural	280	61.75	12.29	19.90		
					12.37	1.05*
Urban	120	74.68	12.54	16.79		

*Not Significant at 0.5 level

A close look at the mean scores provided in table 4.10 indicates that the mean scores for rural and urban areas stood at 61.75 and 74.68 respectively. The standard deviation for rural and urban students stood respectively at 12.29 and 12.54, indicating more dispersion experienced in the case of urban students than that of the rural students. The coefficient of variation stood at 19.90 per cent and 16.79 per cent respectively for the rural and urban areas. The calculated value obtained for the means is 1.05. A comparison of the calculated value with that of the table value indicates that the calculated value is lower than the table value and hence the null hypothesis that "There is no significant difference between the means of the Reading Speed scores of rural and urban students taught through Conventional Teaching Method as measured by Post test" has been accepted.

Null Hypothesis: 11 (H_o11)

There is no significant difference between the means of the Gain Scores of boys and girls of Conventional Method Group in Reading Speed.

In order to establish the identity of the Control Group with regard to sex as the variable, the H_o11 was formulated. In order to test this Null Hypothesis, 't' test was attempted between the means of the two Sub-Sample Groups namely boys and girls.

Table 4. 11 Significance of Difference between the Means of the Gain Scores of Boys and Girls taught through Conventional Method in Reading Speed

Group	N	Mean	S.D	C.V.	S.E	t
Boys	200	0.99	0.37	37.37	0.68	0.1*
Girls	200	2.30	0.82	35.65		

*Not Significant at 0.5 level

A close perusal of the mean scores provided in Table 4.11 for boys and girls indicates that the mean gain scores of boys and girls between the pre and post tests were 0.99 and 2.30 respectively. The coefficient of variation registered for these two groups indicate a relatively stable scoring for both boys and girls, though the stability is more for boys 37.37 per cent, when compared to girls 35.65 per cent. The 't' value calculated indicates that the differences in the gains are not significant between boys and girls as the calculated 't' value of 0.1 is lower than the table 't' value of 1.96. Hence the null hypothesis is not rejected and it is concluded that there is no significant difference between the means of the gain scores of boys and girls in Reading Speed between the pre and Post-Tests.

Null Hypothesis: 12(H_o12)

There is no significant difference between the means of the Gain Scores of rural and urban students of Conventional Method Group in Reading Speed.

In order to establish the identity of the Control Group with regard to locality as a variable, the H_o12 was formulated. In order to test this Null Hypothesis, 't' test was attempted between the means of the two Sub-Sample Groups namely rural and urban students.

Table 4.12 Significance of Difference between the Means of the Gain Scores of
Rural and Urban Students taught through Conventional Method in
Reading Speed

Group	N	Mean	S.D	C.V.	S.E	t
Rural	280	0.99	0.78	78.79	0.77	1.7*
Urban	120	2.30	0.74	32.17		

*Not Significant at 0.5 level

A look at the mean values provided in Table 4.12 shows that the
mean gain scores of the urban students of the Conventional Method Group
in the Reading Speed between the pre and Post-Tests is relatively higher
with 2.30 when compared to that of rural students with 0.99, implying the
better performance of the urban students than their counterparts. The
standard deviation and the eventual coefficient of variation worked out
also shows a higher instability experienced in scoring by the rural students
than the urban students. However, this difference in the mean scores has
turned out to be insignificant as the calculated 't' value ,1.7 is less than the
table 't' value of 1.96. Thus, this test shows that rural and urban students
do not differ between themselves in terms of their Gain Scores in
Vocabulary between the pre and Post-Tests.

Null Hypothesis: 13($H_0$13)

*There is no significant difference between the means of the
Vocabulary scores of boys and girls taught through Conventional Teaching
Method as measured by Pre-Test*

In order to establish the identity of the Experimental Group with
regard to Post-Test, the $H_0$13 was formulated. In order to test this Null
Hypothesis, 't' test was attempted between the means of the two Sub-
Sample Groups namely boys and girls

Table 4. 13 Significance of Difference between the Means of the Vocabulary
Scores of Boys and Girls taught through Conventional Method as
measured by Pre-Test

Group	N	Mean	S.D	C.V.	S.E	t
Boys	200	2.8	1.45	51.79	1.42	0.07*
Girls	200	2.91	1.39	47.77		

*Not Significant at 0.5 level

A close perusal of the data provided in table 4.13 indicates that the mean scores of the boy and girl students stood at 2.80 and 2.91 respectively, with a coefficient of variation of 51.79 per cent and 47.77 per cent respectively. An analysis of the mean scores and the coefficient of variation of the two groups indicate that the girl students have a slight advantage in the mean scores over their male counterparts. This trend is not found to be present in the case of coefficient of variation, that is, the dispersion in the scores of girl students is slightly higher than the male students. However, their mean score difference is tested for its significance using the 't' statistics. The calculated value obtained for the means is 0.07. A comparison of the calculated value with that of the table value indicates that the calculated value is less than the table value and hence the null hypothesis that" there is no significant difference between the means of the Vocabulary scores of boys and girls taught through Conventional Teaching Method as measured by Pre-Test" has been accepted.

Null Hypothesis: 14 ($H_0$14)

There is no significant difference between the means of the Vocabulary scores of rural and urban students taught through Conventional Teaching Method as measured by Pre-Test

In order to establish the identity of the Experimental Group with regard to Post-Test, the $H_0$14 was formulated. In order to test this Null Hypothesis, 't' test was attempted between the means of the two Sub-Sample Groups namely rural and urban students as measured by Pre-Test.

Table 4.14 Significance of Difference between the Means of the Vocabulary Scores of Rural and Urban Students taught through Conventional Method as measured by Pre-Test

Group	N	Mean	S.D	C.V.	S.E	t
Rural	280	2.84	1.55	54.58	1.43	0.05*
Urban	120	2.91	1.10	37.80		

*Not Significant at 0.5 level

A close look at the mean scores provided in table 4.14 indicates that the mean scores for rural and urban areas stood at 2.84 and 2.91 respectively. The standard deviation for rural and urban students stood respectively at 1.55 and 1.10, indicating more dispersion experienced in the case of rural students than that of the urban students. The coefficient of variation stood at 54.58 per cent and 37.80 per cent respectively for the rural and urban areas. The calculated value obtained for the means is 0.05. A comparison of the calculated value with that of the table value indicates that the calculated value is lower than the table value and hence the null hypothesis that "There is no significant difference between the means of the Vocabulary scores of rural and urban students taught through Conventional Teaching Method as measured by Pre test" has been accepted.

Null Hypothesis: 15 (H_o15)

There is no significant difference between the means of the Vocabulary scores of boys and girls taught through Conventional Teaching Method as measured by Post-Test.

In order to establish the identity of the Experimental Group with regard to Post-Test, the H_o15 was formulated. In order to test this Null Hypothesis, 't' test was attempted between the means of the two Sub-Sample Groups namely boys and girls.

Table 4.15 Significance of Difference between the Means of the Vocabulary Scores of Boys and Girls taught through Conventional Method as measured by Post-Test

Group	N	Mean	S.D	C.V.	S.E	t
Boys	200	4.70	1.45	30.85		
					1.5	0.34
Girls	200	5.21	1.55	29.75		

*Not Significant at 0.5 level

A close perusal of the data provided in table 4.15 indicates that the mean scores of the boy and girl students stood at 4.70 and 5.21 respectively, with a coefficient of variation of 30.85 per cent and 29.75 per cent respectively. An analysis of the mean scores and the coefficient of variation of the two groups indicate that the girl students have a slight advantage in the mean scores over their male counterparts. This trend is not found to be present in the case of coefficient of variation that is, the dispersion in the scores of girl students is slightly higher than the male students. This provides the inference that on the average the performance of girl students in the Vocabulary is better when compared to boys. However, their mean score difference is tested for its significance using the 't' statistics. The calculated value obtained for the means is 0.34. A comparison of the calculated value with that of the table value indicates that the calculated value is less than the table value and hence the null hypothesis that "There is no significant difference between the means of the Vocabulary scores of boys and girls taught through Conventional Teaching Method as measured by Post-Test" has been accepted.

Null Hypothesis: 16 (H_O16)

There is no significant difference between the means of the Vocabulary scores of rural and urban students taught through Conventional Teaching Method as measured by Post test.

In order to establish the identity of the Experimental Group with regard to Post-Test, the H_O16 was formulated. In order to test this Null Hypothesis, 't' test was attempted between the means of the two Sub-Sample Groups namely rural and urban students as measured by Post-Test.

Table 4.16 Significance of Difference between the Means of the Vocabulary Scores of Rural and Urban Students taught through Conventional Method as measured by Post-Test

Group	N	Mean	S.D	C.V.	S.E	t
Rural	280	4.81	1.39	28.90	1.51	0.26*
Urban	120	5.20	1.75	33.65		

*Not Significant at 0.5 level

A close look at the mean scores provided in table 4.16 indicates that the mean scores for rural and urban areas stood at 4.81 and 5.20 respectively. The standard deviation for rural and urban students stood respectively at 1.39 and 1.75, indicating more dispersion experienced in the case of urban students than that of the rural students. The coefficient of variation stood at 28.90 per cent and 33.65 per cent respectively for the rural and urban areas. The calculated value obtained for the means is 0.26. A comparison of the calculated value with that of the table value indicates that the calculated value is lower than the table value and hence the null hypothesis that "There is no significant difference between the means of the Vocabulary scores of rural and urban students taught through Conventional Teaching Method as measured by Post test" has been accepted.

Null Hypothesis: 17 (H_O17)

There is no significant difference between the means of the Gain Scores of boys and girls of Conventional Method Group in Vocabulary.

In order to establish the identity of the Control Group with regard to sex as the variable, the H_O17 was formulated. In order to test this Null

Hypothesis, 't' test was attempted between the means of the two Sub-Sample Groups namely boys and girls.

Table 4.17 Significance of Difference between the Means of the Gain Scores of Boys and Girls taught through Conventional Method in Vocabulary

Group	N	Mean	S.D	C.V.	S.E	t
Boys	200	1.9	0.22	11.58	0.21	1.9*
Girls	200	2.3	0.2	8.70		

*Significant at 0.5 level

A close perusal of the mean scores provided in Table 4.17 for boys and girls indicates that the mean gain scores of boys and girls between the pre and post tests were 1.90 and 2.30 respectively. The coefficient of variation registered for these two groups indicate a relatively stable scoring for both boys and girls, though the stability is more for boys 11.58 per cent, when compared to girls 8.70 per cent. The 't' value calculated indicates that the differences in the gains are not significant between boys and girls as the calculated 't' value of 1.9 is lower than the table 't' value of 1.96. Hence the null hypothesis is not rejected and it is concluded that there is no significant difference between the means of the gain scores of boys and girls in Vocabulary between the pre and Post-Tests.

Null Hypothesis: $18(H_o18)$

There is no significant difference between the means of the Gain Scores of rural and urban students of Conventional Method Group in Vocabulary.

In order to establish the identity of the Control Group with regard to locality as a variable, the H_O18 was formulated. In order to test this Null Hypothesis, 't' test was attempted between the means of the two Sub-Sample Groups namely rural and urban students.

Table 4.18 Significance of Difference between the Means of the Gain Scores of Rural and Urban Students taught through Conventional Method in Vocabulary

Group	N	Mean	S.D	C.V.	S.E	t
Rural	280	1.97	0.16	8.12	0.38	0.84*
Urban	120	2.29	0.65	28.38		

*Not Significant at 0.5 level

A look at the mean values provided in Table 4.18 shows that the mean gain scores of the urban students of the Conventional Method Group in the Reading Speed between the pre and Post-Tests is relatively higher with 2.29 when compared to that of rural students with 1.97, implying the better performance of the urban students than their counterparts. The standard deviation and the eventual coefficient of variation worked out also shows a higher instability experienced in scoring by the rural students than the urban students. However, this difference in the mean scores has turned out to be insignificant as the calculated 't' value 0.84 is less than the table 't' value of 1.96. Thus, this test shows that rural and urban students do not differ between themselves in terms of their Gain Scores in Vocabulary between the pre and Post-Tests.

Null Hypothesis: 19 ($H_0$19)

There is no significant difference between the means of the Reading Comprehension scores of Boys and Girls taught through Reciprocal Teaching as measured by Pre-Test.

In order to establish the identity of the Experimental Group with regard to sex as a variable, the $H_0$19 was formulated. In order to test this Null Hypothesis, 't' test was attempted between the means of the two Sub-Sample Groups, namely boys and girls as measured by the Pre-Test

Table 4.19 Significance of Difference between the Means of the Reading Comprehension Scores of Boys and Girls taught through Reciprocal Teaching as measured by Pre-Test

Group	N	Mean	S.D	C.V.	S.E	t
Boys	200	4.54	0.87	19.16		
					0.8	0.3*
Girls	200	4.78	0.73	15.27		

*Not Significant at 0.5 level

As seen in Table 4.19, the mean scores of Reading Comprehension of boys and girls of Reciprocal Teaching Group stood at 4.54 and 4.78 respectively with a standard deviation of 0.87 and 0.73 respectively. The coefficient of variation indicates that the dispersion is more in the case of boys (19.16 per cent) than that of girls (15.27 per cent). The worked out 't' value indicates that the differences in scores between boys and girls are not significant, as the calculated value of 0.3 is less than the table value of 1.96. Hence, the Null Hypothesis is not rejected and it is concluded that boys and girls do not differ between themselves in terms of the Reading Comprehension scores when they are taught through Reciprocal Teaching.

Null Hypothesis: 20 (H_o20)

There is no significant difference between the means of the Reading Comprehension scores of rural and urban students taught through Reciprocal Teaching as measured by Pre-Test.

In order to establish the identity of the Experimental Group with regard to locality as a variable, as measured by Pre-test, the H_o20 was formulated. In order to test this Null Hypothesis, 't' test was attempted between the means of the two Sub-Sample Groups namely rural and urban students as measured by the Pre-Test.

Table 4.20 Significance of Difference between the Means of the Reading Comprehension Scores of Rural and Urban Students taught through Reciprocal Teaching as measured by Pre-Test

Group	N	Mean	S.D	C.V.	S.E	t
Rural	280	4.54	0.94	20.70		
					0.8	0.30*
Urban	120	4.94	1.04	21.05		

*Not Significant at 0.5 level

A close perusal of the mean scores provided in Table 4.20 for students of rural and urban areas of the study indicates that while for the rural area the mean score registered was 4.54, it was 4.94 in the case of urban area.

The worked out standard deviation shows that it was 0.94 and 1.04 respectively in the case of rural and urban areas. The coefficient of variation was lower with 20.70 per cent in the rural area and 21.04 per cent in the urban area implying that the dispersion in the scores obtained by the students of rural areas were less when compared to urban area. However, the test statistics indicate that the differences in scoring between rural and urban areas are not significant as the 't' value 0.30 was less than table value. Hence, the Null Hypothesis is not rejected and it is concluded that rural and urban students do not differ between themselves in terms of the Reading Comprehension scores when they are taught through Reciprocal Teaching.

Null Hypothesis: 21 (H_o21)

There is no significant difference between the means of the Reading Comprehension scores of boys and girls taught through Reciprocal Teaching as measured by Post-Test

In order to establish the identity of the Experimental Group with regard to sex as a variable as measured by Post-Test, the H_O21 was formulated. In order to test this Null Hypothesis, 't' test was attempted between the means of the two Sub-Sample Groups namely boys and girls as measured by the post-test.

Table 4.21 Significance of Difference between the Means of the Reading Comprehension Scores of Boys and Girls taught through Reciprocal Teaching as measured by Post-Test

Group	N	Mean	S.D	C.V.	S.E	t
Boys	200	28.00	4.1	14.64		
					0.8	0.3*
Girls	200	29.50	5.2	17.63		

*Not Significant at 0.5 level

As provided in Table 4.21, the respective mean scores of boys and girls in the Post-Test in Reading Comprehension stood at 28.00 and 29.50 respectively, with a standard deviation of 4.1 and 5.2 respectively. The coefficient of variation registered for these two groups indicate a relatively stable scoring for both boys and girls, though the stability is slightly more for girls 17.63 per cent, when compared to boys 14.64 per cent. The 't' value calculated indicates that the differences in scoring is not significant between boys and girls as the calculated 't' value of 0.3 is lower than the table 't' value of 1.96. Hence the null hypothesis is not rejected and it is concluded that there is no significant difference between the means of the Reading Comprehension scores of boys and girls taught through Reciprocal Teaching as measured by Post-test.

Null Hypothesis: 22 (H_O22)

There is no significant difference between the means of the Reading Comprehension scores of rural and urban students taught through Reciprocal Teaching as measured by Post-Test.

In order to establish the identity of the Experimental Group with regard to locality as a variable as measured by Post-Test, the H_O22 was formulated. In order to test this Null Hypothesis, the 't' test was attempted between the means of the two Sub-Sample Groups namely rural and urban students as measured by the Post-test.

Table 4.22 Significance of Difference between the Means of the Reading Comprehension Scores of Rural and Urban Students taught through Reciprocal Teaching as measured by Post-Test

Group	N	Mean	S.D	C.V.	S.E	t
Rural	280	27.41	2.65	9.67		
					2.8	1.99 *
Urban	120	31.88	3.13	9.82		

*Significant at 0.05 level

A look at the mean values provided in Table 4.22 shows that the mean scores of the urban students of the Reciprocal Teaching Group in the Reading Comprehension as measured by the Post-Test is relatively higher with 31.8 when compared to that of rural students (27.41) implying the better performance of the urban students than their counterparts. The standard deviation and the eventual coefficient of variation worked out also shows a higher instability experienced in scoring by the rural students than the urban students. However, this difference in the mean scores has turned out to be significant as the calculated 't' value (1.99) is higher than the table 't' value of 1.96. Thus, this test shows that rural and urban students differ between themselves in terms of Reading Comprehension Scores when they are taught through Reciprocal Teaching as measured by Post-Test.

Null Hypothesis: 23 (H_o23)

There is no significant difference between the means of the Gain Scores of boys and girls of Reciprocal Teaching Group in Reading Comprehension.

In order to establish the identity of the Experimental Group with regard to sex as the variable, the H_O23 was formulated. In order to test this Null Hypothesis, 't' test was attempted between the means of the two Sub-Sample Groups namely boys and girls.

Table 4.23 Significance of Difference between the Means of the Gain Scores of Boys and Girls taught through Reciprocal Teaching in Reading Comprehension

Group	N	Mean	S.D	C.V.	S.E	t
Boys	200	23.46	0.70	2.984		
					0.63	2.00*
Girls	200	24.72	0.55	2.225		

*Significant at 0.05 level

A close perusal of the mean scores provided in Table 4.23 for boys and girls indicates that the mean gain scores of boys and girls in Reading Comprehension between the pre and pos tests were 23.46 and 24.72 respectively. The coefficient of variation registered for these two groups indicate a relatively stable scoring for both boys and girls, though the stability is more for boys 2.98 per cent, when compared to girls 2.22 per cent. The 't' value calculated indicates that the differences in the gains are significant between boys and girls as the calculated 't' value of 2.00 is higher than the table 't' value of 1.96. Hence the null hypothesis is rejected and it is concluded that there is significant difference between the means of the gain scores of boys and girls in Reading Comprehension between the pre and Post-Tests.

Null Hypothesis: 24(H$_O$24)

There is no significant difference between the means of the Gain Scores of rural and urban students of Reciprocal Teaching Group in Reading Comprehension.

In order to establish the identity of the Experimental Group with regard to locality as a variable, the H$_O$24 was formulated. In order to test this Null Hypothesis, 't' test was attempted between the means of the two Sub-Sample Groups namely rural and urban students.

Table 4.24 Significance of Difference between the Means of the Gain Scores of Rural and Urban Students taught through Reciprocal Teaching in Reading Comprehension

Group	N	Mean	S.D	C.V.	S.E	t
Rural	280	23.02	1.71	7.43	1.83	2.8*
Urban	120	26.57	2.09	7.87		

* Significant at 0.05 level

A look at the mean values provided in Table 4.24 shows that the mean gain scores of the urban students of the Reciprocal Teaching Group in Reading Comprehension between the pre and Post-Tests is relatively higher with 26.57 when compared to that of rural students with 23.02, implying the better performance of the urban students than their counterparts. The standard deviation and the eventual coefficient of variation worked out also shows a higher instability experienced in scoring by the rural students than the urban students. However, this difference in the mean scores has turned out to be significant as the calculated 't' value 2.8 is higher than the table 't' value of 1.96. Thus, this test shows that rural and urban students differ between themselves in terms of their Gain Scores in Reading Comprehension between the pre and Post-Tests.

Null Hypothesis: 25(H_O25)

There is no significant difference between the means of the Reading Speed scores of boys and girls taught through Reciprocal Teaching Technique as measured by Pre-Test

In order to establish the identity of the Experimental Group with regard to Post-Test, the H_O25 was formulated. In order to test this Null Hypothesis, 't' test was attempted between the means of the two Sub-Sample Groups namely boys and girls.

Table 4.25 Significance of Difference between the Means of the Reading Speed Scores of Boys and Girls taught through Reciprocal Teaching as measured by Pre-Test

Group	N	Mean	S.D	C.V.	S.E	t
Boys	200	67.25	6.10	9.07	3.68	0.05*
Girls	200	68.45	6.01	8.78		

*Not Significant at 0.05 level

A close perusal of the data provided in table 4.25 indicates that the mean scores of the boy and girl students stood at 67.25 and 68.45 respectively, with a coefficient of variation of 9.07 per cent and 8.78 per cent respectively. An analysis of the mean scores and the coefficient of variation of the two groups indicate that the boy students have a slight advantage in the mean scores over their female counterparts. However, their mean score difference is tested for its significance using the 't' statistics. The calculated value obtained for the means is 0.05. A comparison of the calculated value with the table value indicates that the calculated value is less than the table value and hence the null hypothesis that "There is no significant difference between the means of the Reading Speed scores of boys and girls taught through Reciprocal Teaching as measured by Pre-Test" has been accepted.

Null Hypothesis: 26 (H_O26)

There is no significant difference between the means of the Reading

Speed of rural and urban students taught through Reciprocal Teaching Technique as measured by Pre-Test.

In order to establish the identity of the Experimental Group with regard to Post-Test, the $H_O 26$ was formulated. In order to test this Null Hypothesis, 't' test was attempted between the means of the two Sub-Sample Groups namely rural and urban students as measured by Pre-Test,

Table 4.26 Significance of Difference between the Means of the Reading Speed Scores of Rural and Urban Students taught through Reciprocal Teaching as measured by Pre-Test

Group	N	Mean	S.D	C.V.	S.E	t
Rural	280	64.85	6.11	9.42		
					7.26	10.31*
Urban	120	74.85	7.23	9.66		

*Significant at 0.05 level

A close look at the mean scores provided in table 4.26 indicates that the mean scores for rural and urban areas stood at 64.85 and 74.85 respectively. The standard deviation for rural and urban students stood respectively at 6.11 and 7.23, indicating more dispersion experienced in the case of urban students than that of the rural students. The coefficient of variation stood at 9.42 per cent and 9.66 per cent respectively for the rural and urban areas. The calculated value obtained for the means is 10.31. A comparison of the calculated value with that of the table value indicates that the calculated value is higher than the table value and hence the null hypothesis that "There is no significant difference between the means of the Reading Speed scores of rural and urban students taught through Reciprocal Teaching Technique as measured by Pre-Test" has been rejected.

Null Hypothesis: 27($H_O 27$)

There is no significant difference between the means of the Reading Speed scores of boys and girls taught through Reciprocal Teaching Technique as measured by Post-Test.

In order to establish the identity of the Experimental Group with regard to Post-Test, the $H_O 27$ was formulated. In order to test this Null Hypothesis, 't' test was attempted between the means of the two Sub-Sample Groups namely boys and girls.

Table 4.27 Significance of Difference between the Means of the Reading Speed Scores of Boys and Girls taught through Reciprocal Teaching as measured by Post-Test

Group	N	Mean	S.D	C.V.	S.E	t
Boys	200	125	12.45	9.96		
					0.58	15.54*
Girls	200	138	14.29	10.36		

*Significant at 0.05 level

A close perusal of the data provided in table 4.27 indicates that the mean scores of the boy and girl students stood at 125 and 138 respectively, with a coefficient of variation of 9.96 per cent and 10.36 per cent respectively. An analysis of the mean scores and the coefficient of variation of the two groups indicate that the girl students have a slight advantage in the mean scores over their male counterparts. However, their mean score difference is tested for its significance using the 't' statistics. The calculated value obtained for the means is 15.54. A comparison of the calculated value with that of the table value indicates that the calculated value is higher than the table value and hence the null hypothesis that "There is no significant difference between the means of the Reading Speed scores of boys and girls taught through Reciprocal Teaching Technique as measured by Post-Test" has been rejected.

Null Hypothesis: 28 ($H_0$28)

There is no significant difference between the means of the Reading Speed scores of rural and urban students taught through Reciprocal Teaching Technique as measured by Post-Test.

In order to establish the identity of the Experimental Group with regard to Post-Test, the $H_0$28 was formulated. In order to test this Null Hypothesis, 't' test was attempted between the means of the two Sub-Sample Groups namely rural and urban students as measured by Post-Test.

Table 4.28 Significance of Difference between the Means of the Reading Speed Scores of Rural and Urban Students taught through Reciprocal Teaching as measured by Post-Test

Group	N	Mean	S.D	C.V.	S.E	t
Rural	280	128.75	3.85	2.99		
					4.55	1.98 *
Urban	120	137.80	5.25	3.81		

*Significant at 0.05 level

A close look at the mean scores provided in table 4.28 indicates that the mean scores for rural and urban areas stood at 128.75 and 137.80 respectively. The standard deviation for rural and urban students stood respectively at 3.85 and 5.25, indicating more dispersion experienced in the case of rural students than that of the urban students. The coefficient of variation stood at 2.99 per cent and 3.80 per cent respectively for the rural and urban areas. The calculated value obtained for the means is 1.98. A comparison of the calculated value with that of the table value indicates that the calculated value is higher than the table value and hence the null hypothesis that "There is no significant difference between the means of the Reading Comprehension scores of rural and urban students taught through Reciprocal Teaching Technique as measured by Post-Test" has been rejected.

Null Hypothesis: 29 ($H_0$29)

There is no significant difference between the means of the Gain Scores of boys and girls of Reciprocal Teaching Group in Reading Speed.

In order to establish the identity of the Experimental Group with regard to sex as the variable, the $H_0$29 was formulated. In order to test this Null Hypothesis, 't' test was attempted between the means of the two Sub-Sample Groups namely boys and girls.

Table 4.29 Significance of Difference between the Means of the Gain Scores of Boys and Girls taught through Reciprocal Teaching in Reading Speed

Group	N	Mean	S.D	C.V.	S.E	t
Boys	200	57.75	7.8	13.51		
					5.7	1.99*
Girls	200	69.55	5.2	7.477		

*Significant at 0.05 level

A close perusal of the mean scores provided in Table 4.29 for boys and girls indicates that the mean gain scores of boys and girls between the pre and pos tests were 57.75 and 69.95 respectively. The coefficient of variation registered for these two groups indicate a relatively stable scoring for both boys and girls, though the stability is more for boys 13.51 per cent, when compared to girls 7.47 per cent. The 't' value calculated indicates that the differences in the gains are significant between boys and girls as the calculated 't' value of 1.99 is higher than the table 't' value of 1.96. Hence the null hypothesis is rejected and it is concluded that there is no significant difference between the means of the gain scores of boys and girls in Reading Speed between the pre and Post-Tests.

Null Hypothesis: 30 (H$_O$30)

There is no significant difference between the means of the Gain Scores of rural and urban students of Reciprocal Teaching Group in Reading Speed.

In order to establish the identity of the Experimental Group with regard to locality as a variable, the H$_O$30 was formulated. In order to test this Null Hypothesis, 't' test was attempted between the means of the two Sub-Sample Groups namely rural and urban students.

Table 4.30 Significance of Difference between the Means of the Gain Scores of Rural and Urban Students taught through Conventional Method in Reading Speed

Group	N	Mean	S.D	C.V.	S.E	t
Rural	280	63.90	4.01	6.28	3.25	1.99*
Urban	120	62.95	3.10	4.92		

*Significant at 0.05 level

A look at the mean values provided in Table 4.30 shows that the mean gain scores of the rural students of the Reciprocal Teaching Group in the Reading Speed between the pre and Post-Tests is relatively higher with 63.90 when compared to that of rural students with 62.95, implying the better performance of the rural students than their counterparts. The standard deviation and the eventual coefficient of variation worked out also shows a higher instability experienced in scoring by the rural students than the urban students. However, this difference in the mean scores has turned out to be insignificant as the calculated 't' value, 1.99 is higher than the table 't' value of 1.96. Thus, this test shows that rural and urban students differ between themselves in terms of their Gain Scores in Reading Speed between the pre and Post-Tests.

Null Hypothesis: 31 (H$_O$31)

There is no significant difference between the means of the Vocabulary scores of boys and girls taught through Reciprocal Teaching Technique as measured by Pre-Test

In order to establish the identity of the Experimental Group with regard to Post-Test, the H$_O$31 was formulated. In order to test this Null Hypothesis, 't' test was attempted between the means of the two Sub-Sample Groups namely boys and girls.

Table 4.31 Significance of Difference between the Means of the Vocabulary Scores of Boys and Girls taught through Reciprocal Teaching as measured by Pre-Test

Group	N	Mean	S.D	C.V.	S.E	t
Boys	200	7.8	1.42	18.21	0.19	2.63*
Girls	200	7.3	1.33	18.22		

*Significant at 0.5 level

A close perusal of the data provided in table 4.31 indicates that the mean scores of the boy and girl students stood at 7.8 and 7.3 respectively, with a coefficient of variation of 18.21 per cent and 18.22 per cent respectively. An analysis of the mean scores and the coefficient of variation of the two groups indicate that the boy students have a slight advantage in the mean scores over their female counterparts. However, their mean score difference is tested for its significance using the 't' statistics. The calculated value obtained for the means is 2.63. A comparison of the calculated value with that of the table value indicates that the calculated value is higher than the table value and hence the null hypothesis that "There is no significant difference between the means of the Vocabulary scores of boys and girls taught through Conventional Teaching Method as measured by Pre-Test" has been rejected.

Null Hypothesis: 32 (H_O32)

There is no significant difference between the means of the Vocabulary scores of rural and urban students taught through Reciprocal Teaching Method as measured by Pre-Test.

In order to establish the identity of the Experimental Group with regard to Post-Test, the H_O32 was formulated. In order to test this Null Hypothesis, 't' test was attempted between the means of the two Sub-Sample Groups namely rural and urban students as measured by Pre-Test.

Table 4.32 Significance of Difference between the Means of the Vocabulary Scores of Rural and Urban Students taught through Reciprocal Teaching as measured by Pre-Test

Group	N	Mean	S.D	C.V.	S.E	t
Rural	280	6.88	1.32	19.2	1.38	1.67*
Urban	120	9.18	1.51	16.40		

*Not Significant at 0.05 level

A close look at the mean scores provided in table 4.32 indicates that the mean scores for rural and urban areas stood at 6.88 and 9.18 respectively. The standard deviation for rural and urban students stood respectively at 1.32 and 1.51, indicating more dispersion experienced in the case of urban students than that of the rural students. The coefficient of variation stood at 19.20 per cent and 16.40 per cent respectively for the rural and urban areas. The calculated value obtained for the means is 1.67. A comparison of the calculated value with that of the table value indicates that the calculated value is lower than the table value and hence the null hypothesis that "There is no significant difference between the means of the Vocabulary scores of rural and urban students taught through Reciprocal Teaching Technique as measured by Pre-Test" has been accepted.

Null Hypothesis: 33(H$_O$33)

There is no significant difference between the means of the Vocabulary scores of boys and girls taught through Reciprocal Teaching Technique as measured by Post-Test

In order to establish the identity of the Experimental Group with regard to Post-Test, the H$_O$33 was formulated. In order to test this Null Hypothesis, 't' test was attempted between the means of the two Sub-Sample Groups namely boys and girls.

Table 4.33 Significance of Difference between the Means of the Vocabulary Scores of Boys and Girls taught through Reciprocal Teaching as measured by Post-Test

Group	N	Mean	S.D	C.V.	S.E	t
Boys	200	10.42	0.88	8.45		
					0.09	10.21*
Girls	200	11.32	0.99	8.75		

*Significant at 0.5 level

A close perusal of the data provided in table 4.33 indicates that the mean scores of the boy and girl students stood at 10.42 and 11.32 respectively, with a coefficient of variation of 8.45 per cent and 8.75 per cent respectively. An analysis of the mean scores and the coefficient of variation of the two groups indicate that the girl students have a slight advantage in the mean scores over their male counterparts. However, their mean score difference is tested for its significance using the 't' statistics. The calculated value obtained for the means is 10.21. A comparison of the calculated value with that of the table value indicates that the calculated value is higher than the table value and hence the null hypothesis that

"There is no significant difference between the means of the Vocabulary scores of boys and girls taught through Reciprocal Teaching Technique as measured by Post-Test" has been rejected.

Null Hypothesis: 34 (H_O34)

There is no significant difference between the means of the Vocabulary scores of rural and urban students taught through Reciprocal Teaching Technique as measured by Post-Test

In order to establish the identity of the Experimental Group with regard to Post-Test, the H_O34 was formulated. In order to test this Null Hypothesis, 't' test was attempted between the means of the two Sub-Sample Groups namely rural and urban students as measured by Post-Test.

Table 4.34 Significance of Difference between the Means of the Vocabulary Scores of Rural and Urban Students taught through Reciprocal Teaching as measured by Post-Test

Group	N	Mean	S.D	C.V.	S.E	t
Rural	280	10.58	1.61	8.22		
					0.39	2,46*
Urban	120	11.54	1.01	8.75		

*Significant at 0.05 level

A close look at the mean scores provided in table 4.34 indicates that the mean scores for rural and urban areas stood at 10.58 and 11.54 respectively. The standard deviation for rural and urban students stood respectively at 1.61 and 1.01, indicating more dispersion experienced in the case of rural students than that of the urban students. The coefficient of variation stood at 8.22 per cent and 8.75 per cent respectively for the rural and urban areas. The calculated value obtained for the means is 2.46. A comparison of the calculated value with that of the table value indicates that the calculated value is higher than the table value and hence the null hypothesis that "There is no significant difference between the means of the Vocabulary scores of rural and urban students taught through Reciprocal Teaching Technique as measured by Post-Test" has been rejected

Null Hypothesis: 35 (H_O35)

There is no significant difference between the means of the Gain Scores of boys and girls of Reciprocal Teaching Group in Vocabulary.

In order to establish the identity of the Experimental Group with regard to sex as the variable, the H_O35 was formulated. In order to test this Null Hypothesis, 't' test was attempted between the means of the two Sub-Sample Groups namely boys and girls.

Table 4.35 Significance of Difference between the Means of the Gain Scores of Boys and Girls taught through Reciprocal Teaching in Vocabulary

Group	N	Mean	S.D	C.V.	S.E	t
Boys	200	2.62	0.54	20.61	0.35	2.00*
Girls	200	4.02	0.34	8.46		

*Significant at 0.05 level

A close perusal of the mean scores provided in Table 4.35 for boys and girls indicates that the mean gain scores of boys and girls between the pre and pos tests were 2.62 and 4.02 respectively. The coefficient of variation registered for these two groups indicate a relatively stable scoring for both boys and girls, though the stability is more for boys 20.61 per cent, when compared to girls 8.46 per cent. The 't' value calculated indicates that the differences in the gains are significant between boys and girls as the calculated 't' value of 2.0 is higher than the table 't' value of 1.96. Hence the null hypothesis is rejected and it is concluded that there is significant difference between the means of the gain scores of boys and girls in Vocabulary between the pre and Post-Tests.

Null Hypothesis: 36 (H_O36)

There is no significant difference between the means of the Gain Scores of rural and urban students of Reciprocal Teaching Group in Vocabulary.

In order to establish the identity of the Experimental Group with regard to locality as a variable, the H_O36 was formulated. In order to test this Null Hypothesis, 't' test was attempted between the means of the two Sub-Sample Groups namely rural and urban students.

Table 4.36 Significance of Difference between the Means of the Gain Scores of Rural and Urban Students taught through Reciprocal Teaching in Vocabulary

Group	N	Mean	S.D	C.V.	S.E	t
Rural	280	3.12	0.45	14.42	0.5	4.63*
Urban	120	3.80	0.50	13.16		

*Significant at 0.05 level

A look at the mean values provided in Table 4.36 shows that the mean gain scores of the urban students of the Reciprocal Teaching Group in Vocabulary between the pre and Post-Tests is relatively higher with 3.80 when compared to that of rural students with 3.12, implying the better performance of the urban students than their counterparts. The standard deviation and the eventual coefficient of variation worked out also shows a higher instability experienced in scoring by the rural students than the urban students. However, this difference in the mean scores has turned out to be significant as the calculated 't' value, 4.63 is higher than the table T value of 1.96. Thus, this test shows that rural and urban students differ between themselves in terms of their Gain Scores in Vocabulary between the pre and Post-Tests.

COMPARISION OF THE EXPERIMENTAL GROUP WITH CONTROL GROUP

Null Hypothesis: $H_0 37$

There is no significant difference between the means of the Gain Scores of Conventional Teaching Group and Reciprocal Teaching Group in Reading Comprehension.

In order to establish the identity of the whole sample with regard to the control and experimental groups as the variable, the $H_0 37$ was formulated. In order to test this Null Hypothesis, 't' test was attempted between the means of the two Sub-Sample Groups namely Conventional and Reciprocal Groups.

Table 4.37 Significance of Difference between the Gain Scores of the Conventional Method Group and Reciprocal Teaching group in Reading Comprehension

Group	N	Mean	S.D	C.V.	S.E	t
Conventional	400	1.02	0.04	3.92	1.90	12.14*
Reciprocal	400	24.09	3.85	15.98		

*Significant at 0.05 level

A close perusal of the mean scores provided in Table 4.37 for the Conventional and Reciprocal Groups indicates that the mean gain scores of the Conventional and Reciprocal Groups between the pre and pos tests were 1.02 and 24.09 respectively. The coefficient of variation registered for these two groups indicate a relatively stable scoring for both the groups, though the stability is more for Reciprocal Group 15.98 per cent, when compared to Conventional Group 3.92 per cent. The 't' value calculated indicates that the differences in the gains are significant between the groups as the calculated 't' value of 12.94 is higher than the table 't' value of 1.96. Hence the null hypothesis is rejected and it is concluded that there is significant difference between the means of the gain scores of Conventional and Reciprocal Groups in Reading Comprehension between the pre and Post-Tests.

Null Hypothesis: 38 (H_o38)

There is no significant difference between the means of the Gain Scores of Conventional Teaching Group and Reciprocal Teaching Group in Reading Speed.

In order to establish the identity of the whole sample with regard to the control and experimental groups as the variable, the H_O38 was formulated. In order to test this Null Hypothesis, 't' test was attempted between the means of the two Sub-Sample Groups namely Conventional and Reciprocal Groups.

Table 4.38 Significance of Difference between the Gain Scores of the Conventional Method Group and Reciprocal Teaching Group in Reading Speed

Group	N	Mean	S.D	C.V.	S.E	t
Conventional	400	0.025	0.001	3.92		
					7.75	8.21*
Reciprocal	400	63.65	7.32	11.50		

*Significant at 0.05 level

A close perusal of the mean scores provided in Table 4.38 for the Conventional and Reciprocal Groups indicates that the mean gain scores of the Conventional and Reciprocal Groups between the pre and Post-Tests were 0.025 and 63.65 respectively. The coefficient of variation registered for these two groups indicate a relatively stable scoring for both the groups, though the stability is more for Reciprocal Group 11.50 per cent, when compared to Conventional Group 3.92 per cent. The 't' value calculated indicates that the differences in the gains are significant between the groups as the calculated 't' value of 8.21 is higher than the table 't' value of 1.96. Hence, the null hypothesis is rejected and it is concluded that there is significant difference between the means of the gain scores of Conventional and Reciprocal Groups in Reading Speed between the pre and Post-Tests.

Null Hypothesis: 39 (H_O39)

There is no significant difference between the means of the Gain Scores of Conventional Teaching Group and Reciprocal Teaching Group in Vocabulary,

In order to establish the identity of the whole sample with regard to the control and experimental groups as the variable, the H_O39 was formulated. In order to test this Null Hypothesis, 't' test was attempted between the means of the two Sub-Sample Groups namely Conventional and Reciprocal Groups.

Table 4.39 Significance of Difference between the Gain Scores of the Conventional Method Group and Reciprocal Teaching Group in Vocabulary

Group	N	Mean	S.D	C.V.	S.E	t
Conventional	400	2.10	1.58	75.24	0.61	2.08*
Reciprocal	400	3.37	0.44	13.06		

*Significant at 0.05 level

A close perusal of the mean scores provided in Table 4.39 for the Conventional and Reciprocal Groups indicates that the mean gain scores of the Conventional and Reciprocal Groups between the pre and Post-Tests were 2.10 and 3.37 respectively. The coefficient of variation registered for these two groups indicate a relatively stable scoring for both the groups, though the stability is more for Conventional Group 75.24 per cent, when compared to Reciprocal Group 13.06 per cent. The 't' value calculated indicates that the differences in the gains are significant between the groups as the calculated 't' value of 2.08 is higher than the table 't' value of 1.96. Hence, the null hypothesis is rejected and it is concluded that there is significant difference between the means of the gain scores of Conventional and Reciprocal Groups in Vocabulary between the pre and Post-Tests.

Null Hypothesis: 40 (H_O40)

There is no significant difference between the means of the Pre and Post-Test Scores the Reciprocal Teaching Group in Reading Comprehension.

In order to establish the identity of the Experimental Group with regard to the test as variable, the H_O40 was formulated. In order to test this Null Hypothesis, 't' test was attempted between the means of the two Sub-Sample Groups namely Pre-test and Post-test.

Table 4.40 Significance of Difference between the Reading Comprehension Scores of Pre-Test and Post-Test -Reciprocal Teaching Group

Group	N	Mean	S.D	C.V.	S.E	t
Pre - Test	400	4.66	0.80	1.72		
					2.73	8.82*
Post - Test	400	27.85	4.65	16.17		

*Significant at 0.05 level

A close perusal of the mean scores provided in Table 4.40 for Pre and Posts indicates that the mean scores of Pre-test and Post-test for Reading Comprehension were 4.66 and 27.85 respectively. The stability of scoring is more for the Post-Test 16.17 per cent, when compared to Pre-Test 01.72 per cent. The 't' value calculated indicates that the differences in the scores are significant between Pre-test and Post-test as the calculated 't' value of 8.82 is higher than the table 't' value of 1.96. Hence the null hypothesis is rejected and it is concluded that there is significant difference between the means of the gain scores of the pre and Post-Tests in Reading Comprehension.

Null Hypothesis: 41 (H_o41)

There is no significant difference between the means of the Pre and Post-Test Scores the Reciprocal Teaching Group in Reading Speed.

In order to establish the identity of the Experimental Group with regard to the test as variable, the H_o41 was formulated. In order to test this Null Hypothesis, 't' test was attempted between the means of the two Sub-Sample Groups namely Pre-test and Post-test.

Table 4.41 Significance of Difference between the Reading Speed Scores of Pre -Test and Post-Test – Reciprocal Teaching Group

Group	N	Mean	S.D	C.V.	S.E	t
Pre-Test	400	69.85	6.67	9.59		
					10.00	6.17*
Post-Test	400	131.5	13.37	10.17		

*Significant at 0.05 level

A close perusal of the mean scores provided in Table 4.41 for Pre and Posts indicates that the mean scores of Pre-test and Post-test for Reading Speed were 69.85 and 131.50 respectively. The stability of scoring is more for the Post-Test 10.17 per cent, when compared to Pre-Test 9.59 per cent. The 't' value calculated indicates that the differences in the scores are significant between Pre-test and Post-test as the calculated 't' value of 6.17 is higher than the table 't' value of 1.96. Hence the null hypothesis is rejected and it is concluded that there is significant difference between the means of the scores of the pre and Post-Tests in Reading Speed.

Null Hypothesis: 42 (H_O42)

There is no significant difference between the means of the Pre and Post-Test Scores the Reciprocal Teaching Group in Vocabulary.

In order to establish the identity of the Experimental Group with regard to the test as variable, the H_O42 was formulated. In order to test this Null Hypothesis, 't' test was attempted between the means of the two Sub-Sample Groups namely Pre-test and Post-test.

Table 4.42 Significance of Difference between the Vocabulary Scores of Pre-Test and Post-Test - Reciprocal Teaching Group

Group	N	Mean	S.D	C.V.	S.E	t
Pre-Test	400	7.57	1.42	18.76	1.18	2.64*
Post-Test	400	10.87	0.94	8.6		

*Significant at 0.05 level

A close perusal of the mean scores provided in Table 4.42 for Pre and Posts indicates that the mean scores of Pre-test and Post-test for Vocabulary were 7.57 and 10.87 respectively. The t value calculated indicates that the differences in the scores are significant between Pre-test and Post-test as the calculated t value of 2.64 is higher than the table 't' value of 1.96. Hence the null hypothesis is rejected and it is concluded that there is significant difference between the means of the scores of the pre and Post-Tests in Vocabulary.

Difference between the Gain scores of Boys and Girls and Rural and Urban Students Reciprocal Teaching Group in Reading Comprehension

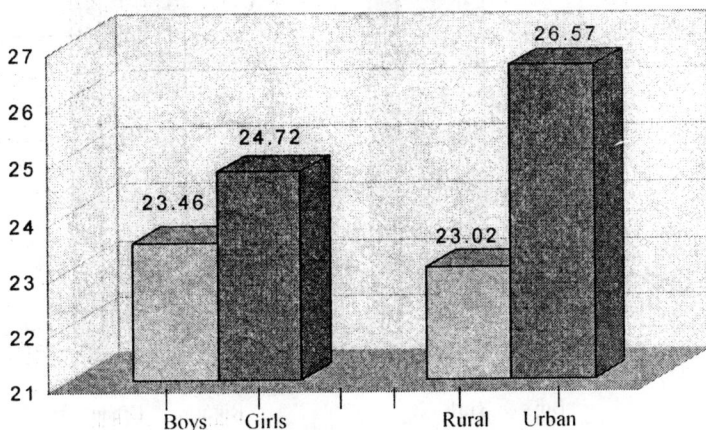

Difference between the gain scores of Boys and Girls and Rural and Urban students of Reciprocal Teaching group in Reading speed

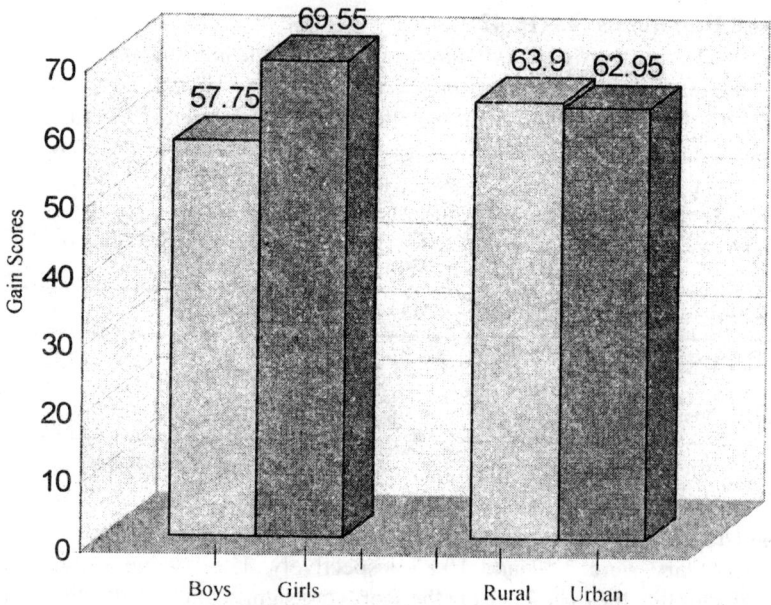

Difference between the Gain Scores of Boys and Girls and Rural and Urban student of Reciprocal Teaching Group In Vocabulary

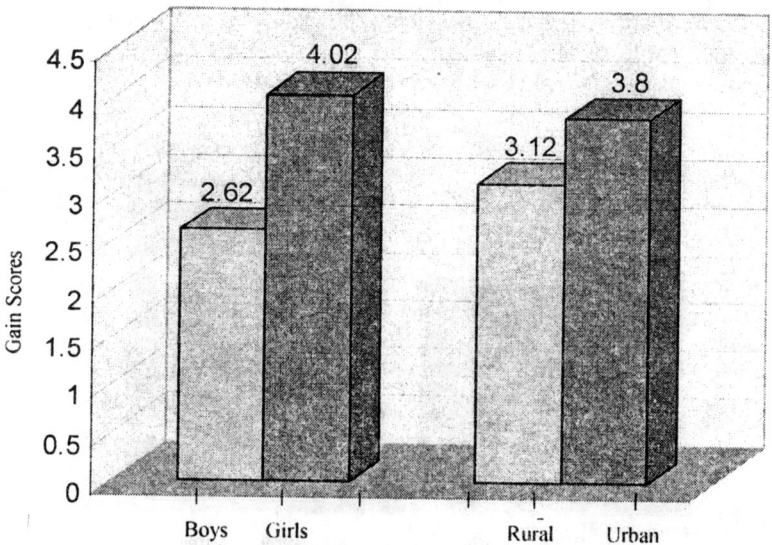

Analysis of Variance

The investigator has made use of the technique of analysis of variance to find out whether there is any significant difference between the means of gain scores of the experimental groups in terms of the variations in the socio economic status.

Null Hypothesis: 43 (H_o43)

There is no significant difference between the means of the gain scores of the Experimental Group students in terms of the variations in the socio economic status.

Table 4.43 ANOVA Table testing the Significance of Difference between the groups in terms of Socio-Economic Status

Source of Variation	d.f	Mean Square	'F' Ratio	Table 'F' Value
Between Groups	2	15.52	2.21*	3.03
WithinGroups	398	7.01		

* Not significant at 5 per cent level.

As the computed value of F, i.e, 2.21 does not reach the critical value at 0.05 level of significance, the null hypothesis cannot be rejected. Hence, it can be concluded that there is no significant difference in the gain scores of the Experimental Group Students in terms of the variations in the socio economic status. This finding reveals that the Reciprocal Teaching benefits all the students irrespective of their variations due to socio economic status.

Null Hypothesis: 44 (H_o44)

There is no significant difference between the means of the gain scores of the Experimental Group students in terms of the variations in their exposure to Newspapers and Magazines.

Table 4.44 ANOVA Table testing the Significance of Difference between the groups in terms of their exposure to Newspaper and magazines

Source of Variation	d.f	Mean Square	'F' Ratio	Table 'F' Value
Between Groups	2	12.91	2.30*	3.03
Within Groups	398	5.06		

*Not significant at 5 per cent level.

As the computed value of F, i.e, 2.30 does not reach the critical value at 0.05 level of significance, the null hypothesis cannot be rejected. Hence, it can be concluded that there is no significant difference in the gain scores of the Experimental Group Students in terms of the variations in their exposure to Newspaper and Magazines. This finding reveals that the Reciprocal Teaching benefits all the students irrespective of their variations in their exposure to Newspapers and Magazines. It can be inferred that even the rural students without exposure to Newspapers and Magazines will be able to get the benefit of Reciprocal Teaching.

Null Hypothesis: 45 ($H_0$45)

There is no significant difference between the means of the gain scores of the Experimental Group students in terms of the variations in their Language interest.

Table 4.45 ANOVA Table testing the Significance of Difference between the groups in terms of their Language Interest

Source of Variation	d.f	Mean Square	'F' Ratio	Wable 'F' Value
Between Groups	2	20.14		
			2.10*	3.03
Within Groups	398	9.57		

*Not significant at 5 per cent level.

As the computed value of F, i.e, 2.10 does not reach the critical value at 0.05 level of significance, the null hypothesis cannot be rejected. Hence, it can be concluded that there is no significant difference in the gain scores of the Experimental Group Students in terms of the variations in their Language interest. This finding reveals that the Reciprocal Teaching benefits all the students irrespective of their variations in their Language interest. It can be inferred that the students with high interest, medium interest and low interest will also be able to get the benefit of Reciprocal Teaching.

Null Hypothesis: 46 ($H_0$46)

There is no significant difference between the means of the gain scores of the Experimental Group students in terms of the types of the Schools.

Table 4.46 ANOVA Table testing the Significance of Difference between the groups in terms of the type of Schools

Source of Variation	d.f	Mean Square	'F' Ratio	Table 'F' Value
Between Groups	2	18.64	1.94*	3.03
Within Groups	398	9.58		

*Not significant at 5 per cent level.

As the computed value of F, i.e. 1.94 does not reach the critical value at 0.05 level of significance, the null hypothesis cannot be rejected. Hence, it can be concluded that there is no significant difference in the gain scores of the Experimental Group Students in terms of the types of schools. This finding reveals that the Reciprocal Teaching benefits all the students irrespective of the types of schools namely, Panchayat Schools, Welfare Board Schools and Private Aided Schools. It can be inferred that the students of all types of schools will also be able to get the benefit of Reciprocal Teaching.

INTERPRETATION OF STUDENTS' RESPONSES TO THE WILLINGNESS SCALE

The success of any educational innovation is dependent on the willingness of students who participate in the innovative experiment. In order to ascertain the willingness of the 400 students who formed the experimental group, namely the Reciprocal Teaching Group (RTG), a willingness scale consisting of 14 items was developed. All the 400 students who participated in the Reciprocal Teaching experiment were administered the willingness scale. As the tool was administered immediately after the administration of the Post-Test, it was possible for the investigator to get the responses to the willingness scale from all the participants. The item wise analysis of the students' responses to the Willingness Scale is given as Table 4.47.

To establish whether differences of distribution of responses are due to chance or represent real differences, the statistical technique, chi-square was used.

Analysis of the Responses to Statement 1

Regarding the statement No.1, *"I will use Reciprocal Teaching Technique in my learning process, even if I am not compelled"*, as many as 48.75 per cent of the students have responded in the positive. It indicates that most of the students are willing to use of Reciprocal Teaching Technique, not only under experimental conditions but also in real life situations.

Analysis of the Responses to Statement 2

Regarding the statement No.2, *"Reciprocal Teaching Technique helps me in improving my Reading Comprehension"*, as many as 46.75 per cent of the students who formed the Reciprocal Teaching Group have answered in the positive. This is an indication that majority of the students have realized the capability of Reciprocal Teaching Technique in improving their Reading Comprehension.

Analysis of the Responses to Statement 3

Regarding the statement No.3, *"Reciprocal Teaching Technique helps me in improving my Reading Speed"*, as many as 42.25 per cent of the Reciprocal Teaching Group students have given positive answers, which indicates that the capability of Reciprocal Teaching Technique in improving their Reading Speed has been well realized by a majority of the students.

Analysis of the Responses to Statement 4

In respect of the statement No.4, *"Reciprocal Teaching Technique helps me in improving my Vocabulary"*, positive responses have been given by as many as 50.75 per cent of the experimental group students. This means that Reciprocal Teaching Technique has been viewed as a technique of enhancing their vocabulary by a majority of the students.

Analysis of the Responses to Statement 5

Regarding the statement No.5, *"I will recommend this technique to my friends"*, mixed opinions have been expressed by the students. As many as 39.75 per cent of the students are willing to introduce this technique to their friends and 41.25 percent of them are not wiling to do the same. An informal interview with the students revealed that the lack of willingness in this regard is due to the misconception that this technique has been simultaneously introduced in all the classes.

Analysis of the Responses to Statement 6

In respect of the statement 6, *"Reciprocal Teaching Technique sessions make learning a joyful experience"*, as many as 49.25 per cent of the students have responded positively. This is an indication that majority of the students find Reciprocal Teaching Technique as a joyful experience of learning.

Analysis of the Responses to Statement 7

Regarding the statement No.7, *"I found myself independent in reading during Reciprocal Teaching sessions"*, a large number of students i.e., 55 per cent of the Reciprocal Teaching Group students have responded in the positive. This endorses the view that Reciprocal Teaching Technique is primarily a technique of promoting learner autonomy.

Analysis of the Responses to Statement 8

Regarding the statement 8, *"The discussions that I have with my friends helped me in understanding the text"*, there has been mixed opinions from the students. The discussions during the RT sessions have been viewed as a contributory factor by 27.25 per cent of the students and as a disturbing factor by 42 percent of the students. As may as 30.75 per cent of the students have been neutral in their stand on this aspect. Taking advantage of the discussions or otherwise is purely a matter of individual difference. As a remedial measure, the students were advised to make use of the discussions for a deeper understanding of the text.

Analysis of the Responses to Statement 9

Regarding the statement 9, *"I find some difficulty in switching over to Reciprocal Teaching Technique from the regular techniques which I am used to"*, almost half of the total number of experimental group students have answered in the negative. This indicates that majority of the students do not experience any difficulty in switching over to Reciprocal Teaching Technique from the regular techniques that they are used to. The reason that can be attributed is the simplicity of Reciprocal Teaching Technique.

Analysis of the Responses to Statement 10

Regarding the statement 10, *"The four stages of Reciprocal Teaching are difficult to pass through"*, a majority of the students, i.e., 54.75 per cent, have answered in the negative. This is an indication that the stages of Reciprocal Teaching Technique are easy to pass through which means easy advancement from one stage to another is in line with the increase of the comprehension of the text.

Analysis of the Responses to Statement 11

Regarding the statement 11, *"The discussions with my friends distracted my attention during the Reciprocal Teaching sessions"*, the responses are consistent to a greater extent with the responses to the statement No.8. A majority of the students i.e., 44.75 per cent are of the opinion that the discussions during the Reciprocal Teaching sessions are helpful to them in understanding the text. This is an indication that the 'reciprocal' aspect of this technique really works.

Analysis of the Responses to Statement 12

Regarding the statement no. 12, *"There is nothing new about the Reciprocal Teaching Technique"*, as many as 46.75 per cent of the students have responded in the negative. This is an indication that the novelty of the Reciprocal Teaching Technique is a motivating factor to the students who practice Reciprocal Teaching.

Analysis of the Responses to Statement 13

Regarding the statement No. 13, *"I find the reading exercises easy after going through Reciprocal Teaching"*, more than fifty percent i.e., 50.5 per cent of the students have responded in the affirmative. This is an indication that the success of the Reciprocal Teaching Technique in making reading an easy academic exercise is well established by the experiment.

Analysis of the Responses to Statement 14

With regard to the statement No. 14, *"Going through Reciprocal Teaching Technique is a time consuming process"*, a large number of participants i.e. 55.5 per cent have answered in the negative. This indicates the participants' attitude to consider the time spent in Reciprocal Teaching sessions as time spent usefully and that they don't view Reciprocal Teaching Technique a time consuming process.

From the forgone discussion, it can be seen that the students' willingness to practice Reciprocal Teaching is high and majority of the students are positively disposed to the practice of Reciprocal Teaching Technique in their content reading sessions. This is in line with the findings of the Bruer (1993).

The chi-square values, which have been found to be at significant at 0.05 level for all the statements of the willingness scale indicates that the distribution represents real differences and that the differences are not due to chance.

Table 4.47 Item Wise Analysis of Students Responses to the Willingness Scale

(Y - Yes; U - Undecided; N - No)

No	Statement	Responses			
		Y	U	N	x^2
1.	I will use Reciprocal Teaching Technique in my learning process, even if I am not compelled	195 (48.75%)	110 (27.5%)	95 (23.75%)	43.63*
2.	Reciprocal Teaching Technique helps me in improving my Reading Comprehension	187 (46.75%)	84 (21%)	129 (32.25%)	40.00*
3.	Reciprocal Teaching Technique helps me in improving my Reading Speed	169 (42.25%)	119 (29.75%)	112 (28%)	14.45*
4.	Reciprocal Teaching Technique helps me in improving my Vocabulary	203 (50.75%)	102 (25.5%)	95 (23.75%)	54.79*
5.	I will recommend this technique to my friends	159 (39.75%)	76 (19%)	165 (41.25%)	37.12*
6.	Reciprocal Teaching Technique sessions make learning a joyful experience	197 (49.25%)	108 (27%)	95 (23.75%)	46.24*
7.	I found myself independent in reading during Reciprocal Teaching sessions	222 (55.5%)	92 (23%)	86 (21.5%)	88.58*
8.	The discussions that I had with my friends helped me in understanding the text	109 (27.25%)	123 (30.75%)	168 (42%)	14.26*
9.	I find some difficulty in switching over to Reciprocal Teaching Technique from the regular techniques which I am used to	58 (14.5%)	143 (35.75%)	199 (49.75%)	75.61*
10.	The four stages of Reciprocal Teaching are difficult to pass through	60 (15%)	121 (30.25%)	219 (54.75%)	96.52*
11.	The discussions with my friends distracted my attention during the Reciprocal Teaching sessions	87 (21.75%)	134 (33.5%)	179 (44.75%)	31.75*
12.	There is nothing new about the Reciprocal Teaching Technique	114 (28.5%)	99 (24.75%)	187 (46.75%)	33.25*
13.	I find the reading exercises easy after going Through Reciprocal Teaching	202 (50.5%)	125 (31.25%)	73 (18.25%)	63.19*
14.	Going through Reciprocal Teaching Technique is a time-consuming process	82 (20.5%)	97 (24.25%)	221 (55.25%)	87.31*

* indicates x^2 values that are significant at 0.05 level

INTERPRETATION OF TEACHERS' RESPONSES TO THE WILLINGNESS SCALE

The willingness scale was administered to the ten teachers who handled the Reciprocal Teaching classes in the ten schools taken for the study.

The item wise analysis of the teachers' responses to the willingness scale is given in the table 4.48. A perusal of the overall responses of the teachers indicate a high level of willingness on the part of the teachers to implement Reciprocal Teaching Technique in their class room situations. They also reveal their willingness to accept the salient features and the strategies of the Reciprocal Training Technique.

As shown in the table 4.48, simple percentage analysis was done for each of the teachers' responses. On the basis of the analysis of the opinions expressed by the students, the following conclusions could be drawn:

1.   The objectives Reciprocal Teaching are clear to as many as eighty percent of the teachers.

2.   The strategies involved in Reciprocal Teaching are clearly known to all the participating teachers.

3.   As many as eighty percent of the teachers were very clear about the methodology of the Reciprocal Teaching Technique.

4.   The effectiveness of Reciprocal Teaching is endorsed by eighty percent of the teachers.

5.   The theory underlying Reciprocal Teaching is not clear just to ten percent of the teachers

6.   As many as seventy percent of the teachers have full faith in educational innovation.

7.   No difficulties are experienced by seventy percent of the teachers in implementing Reciprocal Teaching.

8.   Only thirty per cent of the teachers find the Reciprocal Teaching a time-consuming process.

9.   As many as eighty percent of the teachers manage to find materials suitable for Reciprocal Teaching.

10.   An encouraging eighty percent of the teachers are willing to implement Reciprocal Teaching in their classrooms with confidence.

11. Only ten percent of the teachers are not sure of Reciprocal Teaching's role in students' reading skills.

12. It is heartening to note that there is no difficulty felt by most of the teachers is implementing Reciprocal Teaching.

13. Most of the teachers find Reciprocal Teaching an innovation, different from the Conventional Method of Teaching.

14. As many as eighty percent of the teachers are of the opinion that information regarding Reciprocal Teaching Technique.

15. As many as ninety percent of the Teachers view Reciprocal Teaching Technique as a means of promoting learner autonomy.

16. Reciprocal Teaching Technique is viewed by most of the teachers as a way of enhancing group cohesiveness among students.

17. As many as eighty percent of the teachers find their job easy with Reciprocal Teaching Technique.

18. The success of Reciprocal Teaching Technique keeping the students involved in the learning process is endorsed by eighty percent of the teachers.

The foregone findings reveal that the teachers who participated in the Reciprocal Teaching experiment are well disposed and willing to a great extent to implement Reciprocal Teaching Technique in their classroom teaching.

Table 4.48 Item wise Percentage Analysis of Teachers' Responses to the Willingness Scale

No	Statement	Response in %		
		Agree	Neutral	Disagree
1.	I know the objectives of Reciprocal Teaching	80	10	10
2.	I know the strategies involved in Reciprocal Teaching	100	-	-
3.	I know how to conduct a Reciprocal Teaching session	80	10	10
4.	I find Reciprocal Teaching more effective in teaching reading	80	10	10

5. I do not understand the theory underlying Reciprocal Teaching	10	10	80
6. I have lost faith in educational innovation	10	20	70
7. Reciprocal Teaching is difficult to implement	10	20	70
8. Implementing Reciprocal Teaching is time consuming	20	10	70
9. The instructional materials for implementing Reciprocal Teaching are not available	10	10	80
10. I can implement Reciprocal Teaching in spite of several limitations	80	10	10
11. The implementation of Reciprocal Teaching can improve the students' reading skills	90	10	-
12. The theory of Reciprocal Teaching is difficult to understand	10	10	80
13. Implementation of Reciprocal Teaching can improve the students' reading skills	10	10	80
14. Reciprocal Teaching is not new as the features of Reciprocal Teaching are found in the conventional methods	80	10	10
15. Research on Reciprocal Teaching should be disseminated for classroom implementation	90	10	-
16. The practice of Reciprocal Teaching will pave way for learner	90	10	-
17. The practice of Reciprocal Teaching will lead to better group cohesiveness among students	80	10	10
18. The Reciprocal Teaching Techniques make my job easy	80	10	10

INTERPRETATION OF THE TEACHERS' RESPONSES TO THE REACTION SCALE

All the Ten teachers who took part in the Reciprocal Teaching Experiment were administered a Reaction Scale.

The item wise percentage analysis of the teachers' responses to the reaction scale is given in the table 4.49. On the basis of the analysis of the teachers' reactions, the following conclusions could be drawn:

As many as eighty percent of the teachers do not find it difficult to understand the processes involved in Reciprocal Teaching.

No difficulties are experienced by seventy percent of the teachers in making their students go through the stages of Reciprocal Teaching.

As many as fifty percent of the teachers find a greater role of the teachers in Reciprocal Teaching.

Ninety percent of the teachers endorse the view that Reciprocal Teaching promotes Peer Group Interaction.

The suitability of Reciprocal Teaching to large classes is upheld by eighty percent of the teachers.

As many as eighty percent of the teachers are of the view that Reciprocal Teaching keeps the students alert, attentive and involved.

Only ten percent of the teachers find it difficult to handle the various strategies of Reciprocal Teaching.

As many as eighty percent of the teachers feel that the rules of Reciprocal Teaching do not curtail the students' freedom.

The time involved in Reciprocal Teaching Technique is not taken as a negative aspect by eighty percent of the teachers.

Reciprocal Teaching Technique is viewed as a technique that leads to thorough understanding of the text by all the students.

As many as seventy percent of the teachers are of the view that Reciprocal Teaching is a way of providing learner autonomy.

The suitability of Reciprocal Teaching to the present day curriculum is endorsed by as many as seventy percent of the teachers.

As many as ninety percent of the teachers agree that Reciprocal Teaching Technique discourages rote learning on the part of the students.

Regarding the questioning ability of the students, as many as ninety percent of the teachers feel that Reciprocal Teaching elicits specific questions on ideas found in the text.

There are mixed opinions about the maintenance of discipline in the class while prcatising Reciprocal Teaching though as many as fifty percent of the teachers do not feel that maintenance of discipline is not a problem.

The facility of Interactive Learning in Reciprocal Teaching is endorsed by as many as ninety percent of the teachers.

From the foregone conclusions, it can be seen that the reaction of teachers to Reciprocal Teaching is positive to a greater extent and it is evident that Reciprocal Teaching Technique is highly teacher-friendly.

Table 4.49 Item wise Percentage Analysis of the Teachers' Responses to the Reaction Scale

No	Statement	Response in %		
		Agree	Neutral	Disagree
1.	It is difficult to understand processes involved in Reciprocal Teaching	10	10	80
2.	It is difficult to make my students go through the stages of Reciprocal Teaching smoothly	10	20	70
3.	The Teacher's role is reduced greatly in Reciprocal Teaching	20	30	50
4.	Peer group interaction is stimulated when students learn through Reciprocal Teaching	90	10	-
5.	Reciprocal Teaching is well suited to large classes	80	10	10
6.	Reciprocal Teaching makes pupils alert and attentive and keeps them involved	80	10	10
7.	The various strategies of Reciprocal Teaching are difficult to handle	10	10	80
8.	Strict adherence to the rules of Reciprocal Teaching Technique curtails the freedom of the learners	10	10	80
9.	Reciprocal Teaching Technique involves a lot of time	10	10	80

10. Reciprocal Teaching Technique doesn't lead to thorough understanding of the text by all the students	-	10	90
11. Reciprocal Teaching Technique promotes autonomous learning on the part of the students	10	20	70
12. Reciprocal Teaching Technique is not suited to the present day school curriculum	10	20	70
13. Reciprocal Teaching Technique discourages rote learning	90	10	-
14. Reciprocal Teaching Technique elicits pinpointed questions on specific ideas found in the text	70	20	10
15. Discipline in the class room can not be maintained while practising Reciprocal Teaching	20	30	50
16. Reciprocal Teaching facilitate Interactive Learning on the part of the students	90	10	-

REPORT OF THE CASE STUDY

"The individual case stands at the gate way and terminus of generalized knowledge".

"Case study approach is often the best methodology for addressing the critical problems in which understanding is sought in order to improve practice." (Merriam, 1988). Case study is an examination of a specific phenomenon such as a system, an event, a person, a process, an institution or a social group. Case study is a design particularly suited to situations where it is impossible to separate the phenomenon's variables from the context. The table given in the next page lists several case study characteristics from five separate sources.

"A case study is an empirical inquiry that investigates a contemporary phenomenon within its real-life context, especially when the boundaries between phenomenon and context are not clearly evident. The case study copes with the technically distinctive situation in which there will be many more variables of interest than data points, and as one result relies on multiple sources of evidence, with data needing to converge in a triangulation fashion and as another result benefits from the prior development of theoretical propositions to guide data collection and analysis" (Yin.K. Robert, 1994)

Characeristics of Qualitative Case Studies (Merriam, 1988)

Guba and Lincoln (1981)	Helmstadter (1970)	Hoaglin and Others (1982)	Stake (1981)	Wilson (1979)
"thick" description	can be used To remedy or improve practice	specificity	inductive	particularistic
grounded	results are hypotheses	description of parties and motives	multiplicity of data	holistic
holistic and lifelike	design is flexible	description of key issues	descriptive	longitudinal
conversation style format	can be applied to troubled situations	can suggest solutions	specific	qualitative
Illuminates meaning builds on tacit knowledge			heuristic	

The purpose of conducting research in instructional system is two fold - such as bringing about improvement of instruction in varied situations and generating better understanding regarding the inter-relationships of the variables operating in the instructional process leading to theorization. The case study has a significant role to play in attaining both these proposes. Case study in a clinical form can identify the causes of malfunctioning of the instructional system in specific situations and thereby corresponding remedial measures can be proposed. Further, as case study takes a holistic perspective in studying variables operating in real instructional situations, it enhances the understanding of the process of instruction contributing to theorization." (Bruner, 1964). In the studies of Piaget on personality development, there is an assumption that the few individual cases studied intensively represented a larger population to which the findings are generalized.

Sigmund Freud was said to have regretted that his cases read like short stories rather than technical reports. But it is certainly true that Freud's cases had an enormous impact, despite their unconventionality. The case study method which gained momentum through the pioneering case studies of Allport, Freud, Murray, Piaget and Rogers has been recently adopted by Indian researchers.

An in-depth analysis of an outstanding case namely Vijaya

Raghavan (13) who showed significant improvement as a result of his participation in the Reciprocal Teaching Experiment was attempted at by the investigator following all the case study techniques.

Although Vijaya Raghavan's case is only one of many cases of remarkable reading improvement through Reciprocal Teaching Technique, it is presented as a practical guide for the teachers who would be implementing Reciprocal Teaching Technique in their classrooms.

1. Basic Data

Student's

Name	:	**M.Vijaya Raghavan**
Dateof Birth	:	10.08.1988
Age at case study	:	13 years
School	:	Sathamangalam Panchayat
		Union Middle School Lalgudi
Parents	:	Mr.K. Muthukrishan
		Mrs.M. Chandra
Address	:	55-A Paramasivapuram Lalgudi
		Tiruchirappalli Dist

II. Background Information

M.Vijaya Raghavan is a 13-year old boy. He is fair in complexion, thin-built and of medium height. He is a boy of pleasing manners, good rapport with his fellow students and teachers. He does not wear glasses and he has no history of any eye-defects. Born as a single child to graduate parents, he has had his primary education in his hometown in the same school where he is studying currently.

Though, he has always been a high achiever in his earlier classes, his parents and teachers have felt that his reading skill needed improvement.

III. Participation in Reciprocal Teaching and Improvement in Reading Skill.

Vijaya Raghavan was included in the Reciprocal Teaching Training Group and he underwent the Reciprocal Training for twenty days for thirty minutes each. He undertook the pre-test before the experiment and the results indicate an average performance in all the three components of PSK Reading Skill Test. He participated in the Reciprocal Teaching experiment as one of the subjects and he was given thorough training in the four strategies of Reciprocal Teaching, viz., Predicting, Summarizing, Questioning and Clarifying. A model lesson was also demonstrated by the teacher. Though Vijaya Raghavan was nonchalant in his reaction to the experiment in the first week, a remarkable change in his attitude could be observed as the days advanced. He was seen to be more interactive and more involved in the reading classes through Reciprocal Teaching Technique. This involvement led to his taking the role of the 'peer-instructor', leading the group through the various stages of Reciprocal Teaching Technique. A look at the table given at the end of this discussion, which summarizes his performance at three stages of the experiment, would reveal his progress.

His terminal behaviour indicated a more positive and more enthusiastic attitude towards reading, compared with his entry behaviour, primarily due to his better comprehension skill and higher speed in reading.

IV. Home Visit

The home visit was made on a Saturday in the evening hours. Both the parents and Vijaya Raghavan were present. Their house is located in a quite residential area of Lalgudi town.

The parents are in their early forties and have been happily married for fifteen years. The father is self-employed, owning an agency. The mother is a house-maker.

The environment at home is suitable for academic activities. Vijaya Raghavan is provided with access to leading dailies and magazines, besides books for general learning. He has regular newspaper reading habits and he is also in the habit of clarifying his doubts in those news items with which he has difficulties, with his parents. He moves well with the parents and he is equally affectionate to both. The parents are friendly in dealing with him.

Vijaya Raghavan is also given the access to various entertainment programmes that suit his age.

V. Interview With Parents

The parents of Vijaya Raghavan were interviewed by the investigator. Both were happy about his inclusion in the project. Both felt the need for improving his reading skill. The mother was especially happy with his progress and expressed her willingness to be his partner in Reciprocal Reading Sessions at home. His father assured that he would also do his best to share the evenings with him so that Vijaya Raghavan can read text books or general books in consultation with him, using the strategies of Reciprocal Teaching.

VI. Network Analysis

As a part of the case study the investigator observed the progress made by the selected candidates through a systematic and structured observations. Field-notes were taken and entries were subjected to content analysis. The content of the recorded entries were analysed using 'Systematic Network Analysis' technique evolved by Bliss, Monk and Ogborn (1983). The cluster of schemata, which fall under three headings viz., at the start of the Reciprocal Teaching Experiment, midway through the Reciprocal Teaching Experiment, at the end of the Reciprocal Teaching Experiment assist in understanding the impact of Reciprocal Teaching in the various stages of the progress made by the case under investigation (Table 4.50).

VII. Summary and Conclusions

Vijaya Raghavan recorded a significant difference in his performance in the pre and Post-Tests, indicating higher reading comprehension, higher reading speed and higher grasp of vocabulary. His participation in the Reciprocal Teaching experiment has made him an autonomous learner, capable of higher comprehension of ideas in less time and of adjusting his reading speed according to the text type.

VIII. Recommendations and Suggestions

Vijaya Raghavan, with the repertoire of skills that he has acquired during the Reciprocal Teaching experiment, should act as a 'peer instructor' to his fellow-students so that he would be introducing the Reciprocal Teaching Technique to his peers and guiding them in the application of this success oriented reading technique. He also must apply Reciprocal

Teaching Technique in his content area reading and study reading of text books and other such materials related to Science, Social Science etc.,

It is also suggested that he can try decoding meaning from the text in English language also. This suggestion is given on the basis of the general observation that most of the Indian elementary students do not receive good training in reading.

Table 4.50 Network Analysis of A Success Story in Recirocal Teaching

Experiment	At the start of the Reciprocal Teaching Experiment	Midway through the Reciprocal Teaching Experiment	At the end of the Reciprocal Teaching
General			
Motivation	Poor, because of the inability to read and understand	Average, as he finds a way out of his difficulty with reading	High, as he has in hand a successful strategy, which makes reading an easy task for him.
Enjoyment	No enjoyment in reading, as no or very less reading is done	A little of enjoyment out of his interaction with the text and the peers	Great enjoyment ashe finds the reading exercise, to an opportunity learn with his friends in a joyful way
Reading Comprehension			
Predicting	Very poor, as he lacks a holistic vision of the text and the units under which the topic is elaborated	Partially Sound. as he shows symptoms of understanding the whole-part differences	% Clear, as he understands the whole-part relationships. main and supporting ideas. etc.
Summarizing	Inadequate. as he lacks understanding of the text	Shows improvement with the advancement in his understanding of the text	Very good, as he clearly understands of the text in terms of the main points. sub-points. examples etc..

Questioning	Unconnected questions, mostly on irrelevant details	Connected Questions related to the text its various to understand	Relevant Questions related to content and which are difficult
Clarifying	Limited and related to the main idea and sub-points technical	Less, butrelated to the areas of difficulty	More and very much related to the phrases of vocabulary which he does not understand
Readina Speed	Average but slow with text of high stage, changes difficulty	Slightly, higher than the previous of his peers speed in with accordance the text type	Very High above the average level
Vocabulary	Too restricted in terms of understanding and use	Better in understanding	Very good at understanding and use of the words in 'context' and technical vocabulary

CONCLUSION

The analysis of quantitative and qualitative data reported in the chapter enabled the investigator to understand the effectiveness of Reciprocal Teaching Technique. This understanding forms the basis of the suggestions and recommendations given in the next chapter.

5
Summary, Findings, Conclusion and Recommendations

This chapter summarizes the work done, discusses the meaning of the research results, addresses the consequences of the results by relating them to the more general conceptual framework of the research topic and makes suggestions and recommendations as to the applications and utility of the research results.

In the previous chapters, the relevant theoretical aspects and different stages of conducting the experiment were presented. This chapter is devoted for presenting the most significant element of an experiment - the outcome. An experiment is evaluated on the basis of the objectives formulated prior to the experimentation, the accurate procedure adopted and the clear outcome of the experiment. In this chapter, the focus of attention is on the results or outcomes of the experiment and implications. The outcomes of any experiment are to be judged on the basis of the purpose or objectives of the experiment. Hence, in the beginning, the objectives are restated, followed by the whole procedural theme of the experiment in a nutshell. This retrospective view of the experiment is helpful to conceive the outcome from its absolute essence.

RESTATEMENT OF THE OBJECTIVES

The main objective of the present experimental study was to find out the effectiveness of Reciprocal Teaching of reading over the conventional method of teaching reading to the students of 8th Standard. The experiment was designed and carried out to find out answers to the following questions:

1. Is there any advantage in favour of the experimental or control group with regard to the comparison of reading improvement at the elementary level?

2. Is there any significant difference in the reading comprehension level as a result of Reciprocal Teaching, of the sub-samples based on Sex, Locality, Type of Management, Socio-Economic Status, Exposure to Newspapers and Magazines and Language Interest?

Finding answers to the above questions required the formulation of specific objectives for the experiment in a more precise, research-oriented style as given below:

1. To compare the mean scores of Experimental Group and Control Group in the sub tests on Reading Comprehension, Reading Speed and Vocabulary.

2. To qualitatively analyze the effect of Reciprocal Teaching Technique on teachers and students.

3. To offer suggestions and recommendations on the basis of the findings of the experiment.

RESTATEMENT OF THE PROBLEM

At present in the Indian sub continent, where 840 million people use over 1650 languages and dialects including more than 200 classified languages and 18 constitutionally recognized languages of national importance, the role of mother tongue should be appreciated properly. In India, the Central Institute of English and Foreign Languages (CIEFL), the National Council for Educational Research and Training (NCERT) and the Regional Institute of English (RIE) are working towards improving the standard of English. But, there are no such agencies for Tamil in the State of Tamil Nadu. The teachers of Tamil are in a sort of isolation, in the total absence of any professional support from the agencies of education, which gives a closed professional atmosphere and makes it a static system. Though reading skill is given due importance, it is unfortunate that there is no empirical evidence to ascertain the effectiveness of Reciprocal Teaching in the Indian cultural context in mother tongue at elementary level. In line with the above issues and concerns, the present study entitled "Reciprocal Teaching as a Technique of Improving Reading in Tamil at the Elementary Level" was undertaken.

RESTATEMENT OF THE RATIONALE FOR THE STUDY

Studies abstracted in the six surveys of research in Education (1974, 1979, 1986, 1991, 1996 and 2000) revealed that no study has been conducted in India to test the effectiveness of Reciprocal Teaching Technique for improving reading at the elementary level. In this sense, the present study was unique against the series of studies covered in the review.

From the review of literature, the investigator understood that a substantial body of empirical studies done abroad in countries like U.S.A. and Canada found that Reciprocal Teaching had significant advantages as a reading improvement strategy. However, in the Indian context, the potentiality of Reciprocal Teaching as a reading improvement strategy needed to be tested against empirical data of actual research findings.

A look back into all the researches done with regard to Reciprocal Teaching brought out the gaps and overlaps and helped the investigator in identifying the research gap. The investigator took a planned effort to fill this research gap.

The studies reviewed were mainly helpful in developing the method and procedure adopted in the present study. A notable feature was that in the extensive literature reviewed in the present study, there had been no recorded evidence of any research work having been carried out on Reciprocal Teaching as a Technique for Improving Reading Skill at the Elementary Level. It was in this context that the present study became important and essential as endorsed by the specific concerns of earlier researchers.

METHODOLOGY

Pre-test Post-test Equivalent-Groups Design was adopted for the study in which the participants were randomly assigned either the experimental group or the control group.

Two intact groups of Std. VIII pupils from two classes each in Ten elementary schools were taken as experimental group and control group. Due representation was given to rural-urban locality of the schools, type of management and sex of the students. One group was treated as Reciprocal Teaching Group (RTG), which was taught through reciprocal teaching technique. The other group was treated as Conventional Method Group (CMG), which was taught through conventional method of teaching.

The experiment was conducted on a sample of 800 students of Std. VIII from ten elementary schools in Lalgudi Educational District of Tamil Nadu State. Experimental interferences like Mortality, History, Maturation, Interaction of Selection and Treatment and Hawthorne Effect were taken care of in the research design. The results that could be generalized as threats to the experimental research have been minimized to a great extent. Well prepared experimental treatment, valid tools, objective measurement and appropriate analysis enabled generalizations to establish the efficacy of the experimental treatment.

MAJOR FINDINGS OF THE STUDY

From the analysis of the data, it was found that

1. the Reciprocal Teaching Technique contributed to the improvement of Reading Comprehension of the VIII standard students.

2. the Reciprocal Teaching Technique contributed to the improvement of Reading Speed of the VIII standard students.

3. the Reciprocal Teaching Technique contributed to the improvement of acquisition of Vocabulary of the VIII standard students.

4. girls in the Reciprocal Teaching Group recorded higher increase in their Reading Comprehension, Reading Speed and their acquisition of Vocabulary as a result of the treatment.

5. urban students in the Reciprocal Teaching Group recorded higher increase in their Reading Comprehension, Reading Speed and their acquisition of Vocabulary as a result of the treatment.

6. there was no significant difference between the means of the Post- Treatment Reading Comprehension scores of the three socio- economic status groups namely Low, Medium and High.

7. there was no significant difference between the means of the Post- Treatment Reading Speed scores of the three Language Interest Groups, namely Low, Medium and High.

8. there was no significant difference between the means of the Post- Treatment Vocabulary scores of the students from the three different types of schools namely, Panchayat, Government and Private Aided.

9. there was no significant difference between the means of the Post- Treatment Reading Comprehension scores of the three groups, categorized on the basis of exposure to the newspapers, namely Frequent Exposure Group, Occasional Exposure Group and No Exposure Group.

10. there was no significant difference between the means of the Post- Treatment Reading Speed scores of the three groups, categorized on the basis of exposure to the newspapers, namely Frequent Exposure Group, Occasional Exposure Group and No Exposure Group.

11. there was no significant difference between the means of the Post- Treatment Vocabulary scores of the three groups, categorized on the basis of exposure to the newspapers, namely Frequent Exposure Group, Occasional Exposure Group and No Exposure Group.

From the analysis of the responses obtained from the Willingness Scale for the Teachers, it was found that

1. the teachers' willingness to implement Reciprocal teaching is very high, irrespective of the differences in their sex, locality and the type of schools in which they work.

2. most of the teachers (90 per cent) agree that Reciprocal Teaching promotes learner autonomy, increased motivation, high involvement and interactive learning.

3. the majority of the teachers agree that Reciprocal Teaching Technique is an easy and effective Reading Intervention Strategy.

From the analysis of the responses obtained from the Reaction Scale for the Teachers, it was found that1.

1. the majority of the teachers' reaction was very positive towrds Reciprocal Teaching.

2. the teachers find Reciprocal Teaching suitable for large classes as the classes can be divided into small groups for better interaction.

4. the peer group interaction is higher in Reciprocal Teaching sessions than in Conventional Teaching sessions.

5. the learner autonomy is higher in the Reciprocal Teaching Group than in the Conventional Teaching Group.

From the analysis of the responses obtained from the Willingness Scale for the Students, it was found that

1. the willingness of students to use Reciprocal Teaching technique in real life situations is very high.

2. the majority of the students agree that Reciprocal Teaching helps them improve their Reading Comprehension, Reading Speed and their acquisition of Vocabulary.

3. the Reciprocal Teaching sessions are found to be joyful learning situations by the students.

4. the discussions at the various stages of Reciprocal Teaching sessions enhanced the students' comprehension of the text.

The above findings substantiate the findings of earlier research in Reciprocal Teaching abroad by Kelly *et al.* (1994), Alfassi (1988) and King and Parent-Johnson (1990) as given below:

Kelly et al. (1994) assessed the effects of Reciprocal Teaching on the comprehension of poor readers and found significant improvement in comprehension that was maintained after an eight-week follow-up. Another example is a replication study conducted by Alfassi (1988), which investigated the effects of strategy instruction on reading comprehension and concluded that strategy instruction was superior to traditional reading methods in fostering reading comprehension as measured by standardized reading tests.

King and Parent-Johnson (1990) reviewed the experiences they had in involving fifth grade teachers in studying Reciprocal Teaching and found that when teachers consistently and clearly modelled all four strategies, students monitored their comprehension and gained deeper insight into text concepts.

Factors Contributing to the Reading Failure as Identified by the Present Study

Reading is found by many a researcher as an essential instrument in the development of mastery and interest in the content of all the subjects a student comes across. Yet, the present study reveals a disheartening finding that this essential basic skill is not used effectively in the absence of adequate and proper training in the strategies that promote reading and the awareness to minimize and eliminate the retarding factors that impede the speed of reading with sound comprehension.

The importance of the ability to read with accuracy and understanding is unchallenged among teachers, parents and others interested in education. There can be few primary schools in which the acquisition of reading skill is not a major curriculum objective. Reading failure is the result of complex factors whose effect varies between individuals and it is therefore a problem to be treated in terms of individual pupils and their specific needs. However, some generalizations have been made from weaknesses observed in the schools under study in a cross case analysis, which point to contributory causes of reading failure.

Teaching Skill: Though there are many individual exceptions, much more could be done to improve teachers' knowledge of and skill in the teaching of reading. The general level of teaching skill meets the needs of those pupils who learn to read without difficulty, but it does not resolve the problems presented by slow learners and pupils with specific reading difficulties. This is especially evident in elementary schools.

Textbooks: The text books in use meet the needs of the majority of pupils but they are inadequate for slow learners and pupils with specific reading difficulties. Most textbooks have vocabularies and situations, which are not related to the vocabularies and experiences of disadvantaged slow learners. They introduce new words too rapidly and provide insufficient repetition and reinforcement. More serious, the extent and variety of activities and content at the pre-reading stage are, in those reading text-books which offer them, inadequate in assisting slow learners to establish the necessary sub-skills.

Use of Textbooks: Most of the schools observed did little to supplement or extend the activities of the chosen textbooks. Only the textbooks and their content constituted the reading curriculum.

Lack of a Reading Curriculum: There is no basic reading curriculum or organized means of guiding the work of individual teachers. Often this is not an accidental omission but expresses a distinct philosophy of education which leaves each teacher free to develop his/her own work in his/her own way.

Curriculum Weaknesses: There is an undue stress on the early, mechanical stages of reading skill with comparative neglect of comprehension, reading speed and the 'higher' functional skills of reading.

Record-keeping and Continuity: The general level of recording and charting of individual progress is unsatisfactory for the needs of pupils with reading difficulties. Learners' general backwardness in reading is compounded by specific difficulties created within the schools itself by the lack of continuity and follow-up.

Though these inadequacies are in many schools, weaknesses of curricula and method are overcome by the concern and teaching skill of individual teachers. With more rigorous attention to the reading curriculum, many weaknesses can be eradicated and general standards could be raised.

Remedial Teaching Techniques

The following remedial teaching techniques, which have been found suitable by the investigator after the diagnosis of the case study, will hold good for other similar students also.

It is recommended that the teacher

◈ gives directions slowly and in specific steps.

◈ allows the students to consult their friends for clarification or repetition of directions.

◈ limits the amount of written work until the students gain more proficiency in writing.

◈ uses visual aids whenever possible in instruction.

◈ prepares for a new lesson by a brief review of previous material.

◈ provides a daily schedule containing class assignments with space to check off completed work.

◈ structures for twenty-minute work period with as much feed-back as possible.

◈ encourages verbal response in small-group reading sessions.

◈ plans group activities for students with friends and supportive classmates.

◈ provides opportunities for group reporting.

◈ structures questions in such a way that short answers are required.

It is further recommended that the teachers should develop a professional approach. Teacher Centers for a cluster of villages / urban areas are required. Teachers should meet there regularly and discuss problems of schools management, children's behaviour, subject curriculum and evaluation procedures. They should share findings / insights of action research that they may have conducted during the year. In this way, they can break isolation among themselves and get rid of the 'government servant' tag. The center can maintain a small library and subscribe to useful magazines / journals. Use of library books, magazines and newspapers should be encouraged among the students. The Government should allocate separate funds for the regular purchase of reading materials in the school libraries. In this way, primary education can become vibrant at the grassroots in an otherwise dormant school culture.

IMPLICATIONS

Results of the experiment imply that the Reciprocal Teaching Technique strongly influences the outcome of reading sessions in terms of Reading Comprehension, Reading Speed and acquisition of Vocabulary. This implication helps the formulation of some theoretical guidelines so as to modify the present practice of teaching reading at the elementary level.

◈ The major outcome of the experiment highlights the effectiveness of the Reciprocal Teaching Technique in teaching reading. The pupils taught through Reciprocal Teaching have recorded high achievements than their counterparts taught through Conventional Method. In-depth studies conducted by renowned researchers have reported that this is due to the limitations of the traditional system of instruction. Two of the serious limitations of large group instruction namely, lack of catering to individual differences in abilities and lack of uniform attention to all the pupils prevailing in school education system now, can be minimized if Reciprocal Teaching Technique is practised. The friendliness, mutual trust and consciousness of a common goal to achieve and the cohesiveness among members yielded by the Reciprocal Teaching Technique provide a joyful and rewarding learning environment.

◈ The procedure of Reciprocal Teaching warrants changes in the traditional classroom environment. The focus is on improving reading achievement, promoting healthy relationships among pupils of different socio economic backgrounds, developing social skills and self esteem of pupils and providing opportunities for peer tutoring to both high and low achievers. The key element in Reciprocal Teaching is to hold the students accountable for their learning and give them a sense of power and ownership in the ultimate outcome of their learning. The reading tasks provided to the small groups increase the responsibility of the individual member to work for the group goal through shared learning. The limited intervention of the teacher, at moments of need, promotes learning by doing.

◈ For implementing Reciprocal Teaching, sophisticated instructional aids and high-tech electronic gadgets are not required. Any resourceful and committed teacher can adopt this technique in the conventional classroom. This technique can be used both as a complementary and supplementary technique to classroom instruction. The only requirements are a) slight dislocation in the routine time-table of the school and b) change in the seating arrangements in the classroom.

CONCLUSIONS, SUGGESTIONS AND RECOMMENDATIONS

From the quantitative and qualitative analysis of various types of data obtained from the research tools, class room observations, interviews with the teachers and students and expert opinions, the following conclusions emerged.

◈ The Reciprocal Teaching Technique could be used as a mechanism for staff development wherein the text to be read could be read in small groups using Reciprocal Teaching Technique.

◈ The Reciprocal Teaching Technique could be taught to students and parents alike, as regular applications of the technique both in the school and at home would generate positive returns.

◈ Interventional programmes with Reciprocal Teaching technique as the strategy could be arranged keeping in mind the deficiencies of the existing reading skill development programmes. Before one attempts to stem the rot in the system, one has to understand the genesis of the rot and then treat the genesis situation, instead of mechanically stemming the rot. In other words, intervention programmes have to be diagnostic and curative rather than penal and mechanical.

❖ The Reciprocal Teaching Technique could be taken up by the staff development agencies like National Council for Educational Research and Training (NCERT) at the national level, State Councils for Educational Research and Training (SCERTs) at the state level and District Institutes of Educational Training (DIETs) at the district level as an important component of in-service training programmes to ensure a widespread application of this technique by elementary school teachers across the nation.

❖ The National Council for Teacher Education (NCTE) could take steps to include Reciprocal Teaching Technique as a component of the Teacher Education curriculum, in practice in India.

❖ Reading is not specific exclusive to the language teachers. It is the responsibility of every teacher, sciences or social sciences, to deliberately focus their attention on this basic skill which will enhance and accelerate the understanding and comprehension stages on the cognitive ladder. It is stressed and strongly recommended that educators bestowing attention to the ills and maladies of acquisition of Speed Reading with Comprehension should propose programmes and activities in the curriculum which ensure the fundamentally required skills of Speed Reading.

SUGGESTIONS FOR FURTHER RESEARCH

The findings of the present study open up a few areas for further investigation. A few indications regarding the type of further research urgently needed are presented in the following passages.

The present experiment on Reciprocal Teaching is delimited to selected units of reading passages. Future experimental studies can be expanded covering other content areas of Reading viz., Social Science, Science.

Investigators should be encouraged to take up investigations, taking into consideration teaching time and teacher as reference factors as they have far reaching implications in an experimental setting.

The investigator's own experiment with Reciprocal Teaching Technique as described in this research report gives testimony to the effectiveness of the Reciprocal Teaching Technique for improving Reading at the elementary level. Action Research Projects are suggested to be undertaken on large scale, which would promote a better understanding and application of the Reciprocal Teaching. Bridging Research and Development could be one of the effective strategies for such action Research Projects.

PARTING REMARKS . . .

The study is first of its kind in India and has been undertaken due to a quest to contribute to the cause of upgrading the standards of elementary education in India. The present study has clearly demonstrated that Reciprocal Teaching is an effective intervention technique, simplistic enough for implementation at the elementary level and provides an effective model which could be used to teach parents also how to help promote Reading Comprehension among the elementary level students. The Reciprocal Teaching Technique could be capitalized on a variety of fronts through parents, teachers and students. The present investigation offers not only an experiment on the effectiveness of Reciprocal Teaching, but also suggests a technology for enhancing the academic achievement of pupils at the elementary level.

Though the experiment is an end in itself, the study paves way for a new beginning.

BIBLIOGRAPHY

Adler, M.J. 1982. The Paideia Proposal: An educational manifesto. New York, Macmillan.

Ahuja G.C & Pramila Ahuja, 1987. How to increase your Reading Speed, New Delhi, Sterling Publishers Pvt.Ltd.

Alfassi, M. 1998. Reading for meaning: the efficiency of reciprocal teaching in fostering reading comprehension in high-school students in remedial reading classes. *American Educational Research Journal* (Washington, DC), Vol. 35, No.2, P.309-32.

Anderson, R. 1980. Cognitive Psychology and its Implications. NewYork, W.H. Freeman & Co.

Armstrong, D.G., Savage, T.V. 1990. Secondary Education: an Introduction. II ed. New York, Macmillan.

Ausubel, D.P. 1978. Defense of Advance Organizers: A reply to the critics, Review of Educational Research, 48, pp. 251-257.

Bakhtin, M.M. 1981. The Dialogic Imagination, Austin, University of Texas Press.

Bartonb, J. & Calfer, R. 1989. Theory becomes Practics: One Programme, *Content area Reading and Learning: Instructional Strategies,* pp. 366-378, Engleweood cliffs, N.J. Prentice hall.

Best, John W. 1986. Research in Education, VII ed., New Delhi, Prentice-Hall of India Pvt Ltd. Bond Guy and Miles Tinker, 1957. Reading Difficulties: their diagnosis and correction, New York, Appleton Century Crafts, Inc.

Brown P.J. & S.B. Hirst,. (1983) 'Writing Reading Courses'. *Language Teaching Projects for the Third World,* Oxford: Pergammon: 139,

Brown, P.J. & S.B. Hirst, (1983) Writing World. Oxford: Pergammon Press.

Bruner, J.S. (1964) Towards a Theory of Instuction, Cambridge: Harward University Press.

Bruer, J. (1993) The Mind's Journey from Novice to Expert. Washington: American Educator.

Brumfit, C.J. (1980) Problems and Principles in English Teaching, Oxford: Pergammon Press, 4.

Buch, M.B. (1974) A Survey of Research in Education, Baroda:CASE, M.S. University.

Buch, M.B. (1979) Second Survey of Research in Education, Baroda:CASE, M.S. University.

Buch, M.B. (1983) Third Survey of Research in Education, Baroda:CASE, M.S. University.

Buch, M.B. (1991) Fourth Survey of Research in Education, New Delhi: NCERT.

Buch, M.B. (1997) Fifth Survey of Research in Education, New Delhi: NCERT.

Byndrian, G. (1994) 'Highland Park highlights: facts, figures, history, comment', Highland Park: MI, Highland Park Schools.

Calfee, R. (1984) Applying Cognitive Psychology to Educational Practice: The Mind of the Reading Teacher, Annals of Dyslexia, 34: 219-240.

Carter, C. (1993) High hopes, high expectations, high student achievement and development framework for improving educational quality in Highland Park Public Schools, Highland Park.

Carter, Carolyn J. (1997) 'Why reciprocal teaching'. *Educational Leadership*. 54: 6.

Cheney, L.V. (1987) American Memory, Washington: National Endowment for the Humanities. Committee for Economic Development. (1985) Investing in our children, New York: Committee Report. Committee for Economic Development. (1987) Children in Need, New York: Committee Report.

Conyers, J. Jr. (1954) Highland Park report. Washington: House of Representatives, Mimeo.

Cooper, H.M. (1984) The Integrative Research Review: A Systematic Approach. Newbury Park: Sage publishers.

Cubage., & Lincoln Y.S. (1981) Effective Evaluation, San Francisco: Jossey - Bass Publishers.

Dash. M. (1991) "Analysis of Cognitive and Speech Related Processes in Relation to Reading Efficiency and iQ', M.Phil, Psy. Utkal University, in *Educational Research Innovations,* 1988-1992.

Dave, Meeta. (1992) 'An Investigation into Reading Comprehension of the Pupils of Grade VII by Using the Standardized Tests in Gujarat', Ph.D., Education, Gujarat University.

Deb Madhyu and Grewal, Hirdaipal. (1990) 'Relationship between Study Habits and Academic Achievement of Under Graduate Home Science Final Year Students', *Indian Educational Review. 25.*

Devanathan, S. (1988) 'A study of Reading skills in Tamil of pupils studying 5th and 8th standards' Ph.D. Degree of the University of Madras.

Downing, J and Leong, C.K. (1982) Psychology of Reading, New York: A Macmillan.

Ebel, R.L (1979) Encyclopedia of Educational Research, London: The Macmillan Company. Educating Americans for the 21st Century, Washington: National Science Foundation.

Education Commission of the States. (1993). Task Force on Education for Economic Growth. Action for excellence. Denver: Education Commission of the States.

Epstein, Joycee,C. (1984) ' Effects of Teacher Practices of Parent Involvement Change in Student Achievement in Reading and Math', Eric, 20:198.

F. Smith, (1988) Reading , London: Cambridge.

Finn, C.E. Jr, Ravitch, D. (1987) 'What do our 17 year-olds know: A Report on the first national assessment of history and literature'. New York: Harper and Row.

Fisher, R.A. and Mangham. (2002) Statistics in Psychology and Education, New Delhi.

Foss, D.J. (1988) 'Experimental Psycholinguistics', *Annual Review of Psychology,* 301-348.

Fuller, Edwards and Gorman. (2001) 'Rediscovering Practical Reading Activities' in *Journal of Research in Reading,* United Kingdom Reading Association. Oxford: Blackwell Publishers.

Garrett, H.E. (1971) 'Statistics in Psychology and Education', Bombay: Vakils, Feffer and Simon.

Goodman, K. (1988) 'Reading: A Psycholinguistic Game'. *Journal of the Reading Specialist.*

Goodman, K. (1988) 'The reading process', *Interactive approaches to second language learning,* London: Cambridge.

Graff, (2001) 'Rediscovering Practical Reading Activities' in *Journal of Research in Reading*. United Kingdom Reading Association. Oxford: Blackwell Publishers.

Gray, W.S. (1960) *Encyclopedia of Educational Research*, New York: Macmillan Co, 1086 - 135.

Gray, W.S. (1956) *Encyclopedia of Educational Research*, New York: The Macmillan Co.

Greg Brooks. (1984) 'Nineteenth and Twentieth - Century Model of L2 Reading', *Reading for Professional Purposes: Studies and Practices in Native and Foreign Languages*, London: Heinemann.

Hafner, Lawrence E., *et al.*, (1972) Patterns of Teaching Reading in the Elementary School. New York: The Macmillan Company. 177.

Harris and David, P. (1974) Testing English as a second language. Bombay: Tata McGraw Hill Publishing Co. Ltd.

Hathaway, E. (1946) History of Highland Park. Highland Park: High/and Park Board of Education.

Hewitt, G. (1995) Toward student autonomy in reading: reciprocal teaching, 33.

Hillsdale, N.J., (1987) Reciprocal teaching of comprehension fostering and monitoring activities, Cognition and Instruction, 1,2:111-75.

Holmes Group. (1986) Tomorrow's teachers. East Lansing, Holmes Group.

Jandhyala B. Tilak. (1987) The Economics of Inequality in Education. New Delhi: Sage Publications.

Jandhyala B. Tilak. (1984) Urban Bias and Rural Neglect in Education: A study on Rural-Urban Disparities in Education in Andhra Pradesh, 17: 61-86.

Janette Kettmann, *et.al.*, (1996) 'Reciprocal Teaching of Reading Comprehension Strategies for Students with Learning Disabilities who use English as a Second Language', *The Elementary School Journal*, 96.

Johnston and *et al.*, (1987) The Influence of Phonology on Good and Poor Readers when Reading for Meaning', *Journal of Memory and Language*, 26(1), 57-68.

Kamalamani & Mani. (2002) Correlates of School Achievement in Coimbatore District, Coimbatore: Ph.D. Thesis, Bharathiar University.

Kapoor, (1988) 'Analysis of Personal Earnings and Sex Differentials in the Industrial Sector in Punjab', *Indian Journal of Quantitative Economics*, 4, 21-40.

Karpaga Kumaravel, R. (1993) Instructional Technology in English at the Higher Secondary Stage: A system Analysis Perspective, Karaikudi: Ph.D. Thesis, Alagappa University.

Karpaga Kumaravel & Gopalan. (1997) A study of Reading Skills in Tamil among the High School Students, M.Phil Thesis, Coimbatore: SRKV College of Education.

Kelley, T.L. (1969)' A selection of upper and lower groups for the validation of test items'. Washington: *Journal of Educational Psychology,* 30:17-24.

Kelly, M., *et al.,* 1994 Reciprocal teaching in a regular primary school classroom. *Journal of Educational Research,* Washington: 88: 53-61.

Keppel, Francis. (1964) 'Research, Educations Neglected Hope', *Journal of Readin.*

Klitghard and Hall. (1974) Scholl Effectiveness in Karpagakumaravel: Instructional Technology in English at the Higher Secondary Stage: A system Analysis Perspective, Karaikudi: Ph.D. Thesis, Alagappa University.

Kuppuswamy, B. (1968) Research Needs in Educational Psychology, in Uday Shanker and S.P. Ahluwalia, Kurukshetra: Kurukshetra University Books, 155-163.

Leininger. (1985) Qualitative Analysis in Educational Research Innnovations 1988-1992.

Linn, R.L. and Dunbar, S.B. (1990) The nation's report card goes home: good news and bad about trends in achievement. Bloomington: Phi delta Kappan.

Manimekalai, M. (1997) 'Communication Skills in Tamil among the +2 students'. *Journal of Educational Research and Extension,* Coimbatore: SRKV,33.

Marvin, C. Alkin. (1992) Cognitive Science, *Encyclopedia of Educational Research,* New York: Macmillan Co,. 3: 1075-1085.

Marvin, Calm. (1992) *Encyclopedia of Educational Research,* New York: Macmillan Co,.

Masson, Michael, E. (1993) 'Episodically Enhanced Comprehension Fluency Special'. *Psychology,* 47:2.

Masterson, *et al.,* (1992) 'Beginning Reading with Phonology', *British Journal of Psychology,* 83.

Mc Ghee, Paul E. *et al.*, (1990) 'The Role of Cognitive Factors in Children's Metaphor and Humorous Comprehension'. *International Journal of Human Research.*

McKnight, C.C., *et al.*, (1987) 'The Underachieving curriculum: assessing U.S. school mathematics for an international perspective', Campaign: Stipes Publishing Co.

Mehta, G.S. (1989) 'Education, Employment and Earning: The Extent of Disadvantages Against Women, Man and Development, 20-34,

Meichenbaum, D. (1985) 'Teaching thinking: A Cognitive behavioural perspective. Thinking and Learning Skills, Research and open questions', Austin: Society for learning Disabilities and Remedial Education.

Merriam, & Simpson. (1984) Second Language Research Methods, Oxford: Oxford University Press.

Merriam, Sharn, B. (1988) Case Study Research in Education, San Francisco: Josssey Bass publishers.

Michael Stubbs Collinge, N.E. (1990) 'Language in Education', An *Encyclopedia of Language,* 571-575.

Mill, J.S. (2000) Methodology of Educational Research, in Lokesh Koul. New Delhi:Vikas Publishing House.

Miller, D., and Linn, R. (1989) 'International retention and achievement rates'. *Journal of research in Mathematics Education, Reston,* 20: 28-40.

Moore, Phil. (1986) Using Computers in English - A critical Guide. London: Methuen & Co.

Moore, T.W. (1974) Educational Theory:An Introduction. London: Routledge.

Murphy, J. (1990) The Educational Reform Movement of the 1980's: Perspectives and Cases. Berkeley: CA McCuthchan Publishing Corp.

National Commission on Excellence in Education. (1983) A nation at risk: the imperative for educational reform, Washington: Government Printing Office.

National Commission on Excellence in Educational Administration.

(1987) Leaders for an America's school. Tempe: University

(1988) Council on Educational Administration.

National Governors' Association. Center for Policy Research. (1986)

Time for results, Washington: Center for Policy Research, National Governors' Association.

NCERT., (2001) Sixth Survey of Research in Education, Baroda: CASE.

Olson, (1994) 'Rediscovering Practical Reading Activities' in *Journal of Research in Reading*. United Kingdom Reading Association. Oxford: Blackwell Publishers.

Palincsar, A.S. & Brown, A.L. (1985) Reciprocal Teaching: Activities to Promote Read(ing) with your Mind. *Reading, Thinking and Concept Development: Strategies for the Classroom*, New York: The College Board.

Palincsar, A.S. (1986) Reciprocal Teaching, *Teaching Reading as Thinking*. Oak Brook: North Central Regional Educational Laboratory.

Palincsar, A.S., & Klenk, L.J. (1991) Dialogues Promoting Reading

Comprehension, *Teaching Advanced Skills to at Risk Students*. San Francisco: Jossey-Bass.

Palincsar, A.S., & Perry, N.E. (1995) Developmental, Cognitive and Socio cultural Perspectives on assessing and instructing reading. *School Psychology Review*, 24, 331-344.

Palinscar, A.S. (1984) 'Reciprocal teaching: Field evaluation in remedial and content-area reading'. Washington: *American Educational Research*.

Palinscar, A.S. Brown, A.L. (1986) Interactive teaching to promote independent learning from text. Reading Teacher, 39.

Palmer, H.E. (1920). The Principles of Language Study, London: Oxford University.

Parasnis, H.N. (1990) 'Development of a Problem Solving Ability Test for Students of Standard IX: Independent Study', *Educational Research and Innovations*.

Pearson, P.D., Doyle, J.S. (1987) 'Explicit Comprehension Instruction: a Review of the Research and a New Conceptualization of Instruction'. *Elementary School Journal, 18*.

Peryon, Charleen, D. (1985) 'Proceedings of the Annual Symposium on Reading', *Education Collected Works*, Eric, 20.

Pramila Ahuja & Ahuja G.C. (1991) Learning to Read Effectively and Efficiently, New Delhi: Sterling Publishers Pvt. Ltd.

Pressley, M. Snyder, *et.al.*, (1987) How can good strategy be taught to Children, Orlando: Academic Press.

Rajagopalan, D.S. (1981) A Study of the Relationships of the Selected Variables to Reading Comprehension in English, Ph.D., Thesis, Chennai: Anna University.

Reichard, C.S. & Cook, T.D. (1979) Beyond qualitative and quantitative methods. Programs and systems - An evaluation perspective. New York: Academic Press.

Richard, I. A. (1981) How to read a page. London: Routledge and Kegan Paul press.

Robinson, F.P. (1946) Effective Study. New York: Harper and Bros.

Roger, A. Karifman. (1972) Educational Systems Planning. Englewood Cliffs: Prentice - Hall, Inc.

Roger, Farr. (1970) Measurement and Evaluation of Reading. New York: Harcourt, Brace and World, Inc.

Roger, E.M. & Shoemaker, F.F. (1971) Communication of Innovations - A Cross Cultural Approach. New York: Kogan Page.

Roger, Mitton. (1982) Practical Research, Cambridge: International Extension College.

Rosenblatt, L.M. (1978). The Reader, The Text, the Poem: The Transactional Theory of the Literary Work, Carbondale: Southern Illinois University Press.

Rosenblatt, L.M. (1983) Literature as exploration IV ed., New York: Modern Language Association.

Rosenshine *et al.,* (1996) Teaching Students to generate question- a review of the intervention studies. *Review of Education Research.*

Ruth Wodak, David Corson. (1997) Encyclopedia of Language and Education, Canada: Kluwer Academic Publishers.

Samuels & Michael L.L. Kamill. (1988) Models of the Reading Process, Interactive Approaches to second Language Reading, London: Cambridge University Press.

Schwartz, R. & Raphael, T. (1985) Concept of Definition: A Key to Improving Students Vocabulary, *The Reading Teacher,* 198-205.

Selinger, Herbert, W. (1989) Second Language Research Methods. London: Oxford University Press.

Selvaraj Gnanaguru. (1994) Reading Achievement in Tamil Language, *Journal of Educational Research and Extension,* 30.

Shaywitz, B.A., *et al.,* (1992) Discrepancy compared to low achievement definitions of reading disability: Results from the Connecticut Longitudinal Study. *Journal of Learning Disabilities,* 25.

Shaywitz, S.E *et al.,* (1992) Dyslexia and Reading Ability. *The New England Journal of Medicine.*

Singer, H. (1984) Word Recognition, *Handbook for the Volunteer Tutor,* New York, International Reading Association: *The International Encyclopedia of Education.*

Singer, H.G. (1982) An Integration of Instructional Approaches for Teaching Reading and Learning from Text. *The International Encyclopedia of Education.*

Sizer, T.R. (1984) Horace's Compromise: the dilemma of the American High School. Boston: Houghton-Miflin.

Smith and Goodman. (1992) *Encyclopedia of Educational Research,* New York: Macmillan Co,.

Smith, C.B. (1988) Building a better Vocabulary, *The Reading Teacher,* 238.

Spiro, R.J, *et al.,* (1988) Cognitive Flexibility Theory: Advanced Knowledge Acquisition in ill-structured Domains, *Proceedings of the Tenth Annual Conference of the Cognitive Science Society,* 375-383.

Spiro, R.J., Vispoel, *et al.,* (1987) 'Knowledge Acquisition for Application: Cognitive Flexibility and Transfer in Complex Content Domains', *Executive Control Processes in Reading,* Hillsdale, Lawrence Erlbaum: 177-199.

Stanley, J.C, & Campbell, D.T. (1966) Experimental and Quasi -experimental designs for research, Chicago: Rand McNally.

Stanovich, K.E. (1991) Word Recognition: Changing Perspectives, *Handbook of Reading Research,* New York: Longman.

Stedman, L.C., & Kaestel, C.E. (1987) Literacy and reading performance in the United States from 1880 to the present. Reading Research Quarterly, 22, 8-46.

Stern, H.H. (1983) Fundamental Concepts of Language Teaching. London: Oxford University Press.

Stevenson, H.W. (1997) Children's Learning, New York: Appleton-Century Crofts.

Stevenson. (1977) Reading from Process to Practice, London: Association with the Open University Press.

Subrahmanyam, S. (1981) Some Correlates of Reading Achievement of Primary School Children. Ph.D. Thesis, Tirupati: S.V. University.

Sulzby, E. and Teale, W. (1991) Emergent Literacy, *Handbook of Reading Research,* New York: Longman.

Tickoo, (1998) 'Communication skills in English', Chennai: *Proceedings of the annual Conference of ELTAI.*

Twentieth Century Fund Task Force on Federal Educational Policy (1983) Making the grade. New York: Twentieth Century Fund.

Tyler, (1930). Some Correlates of Reading Achievement of Primary School Children, in Subrahmanyam, S. 1981. Ph.D. Thesis, Tirupati: S.V. University.

Valette, Rebecca, M. (1977) Modern Language Testing. New York: Harcourt Brace, lavanovich Inc.

Venkat Iyer, (1986) Dynamic Reading Skills. New Delhi: Sterling Publishers Private Ltd.

Vygosky, L.S. (1981) The Genesis of Higher Mental Functions, *The Concept of Activity in Soviet Psychology.* Armonld: N.Y. Sharpe.

Witty, P. and H.S.Schaeter. (1936) Hypothyroidism as a factor in maladjustment, *Journal of Psychology.* 377-392.

Yin K. Robert. (1994) Case Study Research : Design and Methods, California: Sage Publications Inc.

WEBSITE ADDRESSES

http://dbs.tn.nic.in/gistnic

http://depts.washington.edu/centerme/recipro.htm

http://exchanges.state.gov/forum/vols/vol33/no4/p29.htm

http://teams.lacoe.edu/

http://tnmaps.tn.nic.in

http://www.ciil.org

http://www.interventioncentral.org

http://www.miamisci.org/

http: //www. ncrel.org/

http://www.ncrel.org/sdrs/areas/rpl-e5vs/collab.htm

http://www.orangeusd.kl2.ca.us

http://www.sdcoe.K12.ca.us/score/promising/tips/rec.html

http://www.suitel01.com/article.cfm/reading/45021